The Communication Equation

Authenticity Plus Connection Equals Engagement

A How-To Guide for Outstanding Communication

Emma Serlin was born in London. She is the founder and director of London Speech Workshop and the creator of the Serlin Method™. She has been regularly featured on Newsnight and BBC Radio and has been interviewed by the Times, The Financial Times, Talk Radio and other press. She has an MSc in Psychology and is a trained life coach. She also trained as an actress at Oxford School of Drama. Prior to working in the field of communication she ran her own theatre company and worked in TV drama. This is her first book.

Acknowledgements

My sincere thanks to Jamie Chapman of London Speech Workshop, who helped me in the creation of the very early stages of the book. Thank you also to Gilly Sharpes and the rest of the London Speech Workshop team, past and present, for being supportive, enthusiastic and committed both to this book, our work and to our continued excellence. And a big thank you to all the clients who have been honest and courageous on their journey, and taught me so much. They are both the source and the raison d'être for this book.

Page of Contents

INTRODUCTION

Good communication can change your life.

GOOD COMMUNICATION CAN HELP YOU get jobs, gain promotions, negotiate the challenges of home life, and strengthen relationships with family and friends. It can help you win arguments without aggression and lose arguments with grace. Would you like to know how to articulate your dreams and inspire others to help you make them a reality? It can help you do that, too.

In short, good communication skills are essential if you want to have fulfilling and productive relationships with other human beings. And because we are social animals – and relationships drive so much of what we do – it's not a stretch to say that good com-munication skills are essential for a happy and prosperous life.

To be a good communicator doesn't mean you have to become talkative if you are not, or be the life and soul of the party. It means that when you do need to communicate – and we all do – you have the ability to communicate with an easy sense of confidence. Even if you are nervous or on the back foot – and no matter who you are, some situations do that to everyone – then by using the tools in this book, you can still be a powerful, confident and engaging communicator.

'But can you teach this stuff?' I hear you say.

'Yes!' is the emphatic answer.

This book will give you tools to slip underneath the skin of powerful communication in English and show you its hidden secrets. You will see just how well these techniques work in practice; the effects are often instantaneous.

You can learn to improve in all these areas:

• Increased confidence when communicating

• Sounding more engaging

• Building rapport

• Using body language to make that powerful first impression

• Sounding more formal

• Overcoming nerves

• Handling difficult conversations

- Improving interview performance
- Giving powerful presentations
- Delivering impactful speeches

I have developed these techniques from a wealth of resources, including my training as an actor and years of working as a theatre director, from my qualifications and experience in psychotherapy, psychology and coaching, and from eight years of running a successful communication skills training company, London Speech Workshop (LSW).

This book benefits from the wisdom of expert communicators such as Marshall Rosenberg, who pioneered a form of communication to deal peacefully with conflict (called 'non-violent communication'), Dale Carnegie, who wrote the classic *How to Win Friends and Influence People*, John Gottman's seven principles, outlined in his *Seven Principles for Making Marriage Work*, and even the Bushido virtues of the Samurai warriors.

The book also includes well-known communication tools, such as active listening, open questioning and vocal projection. However, most of its inspiration comes from observing what is happening when communication simply works: the things we do instinctively when we are in full flow and inspired by things we feel passionate about. At those times – when we are without doubt or fear – we communicate brilliantly. It is this that I have taken apart, analysed and put back together in simple steps, so that you can have that brilliance at your fingertips exactly when you need it. I call this collection of simple tools the Serlin Method™.

Time and time again, my LSW coaching team and I have proved how well this method works. The Serlin Method™ will crack anything that gets in the way of powerful communication, be it fear, bad habits, a strong accent or a lack of confidence.

HOW TO GET THE MOST OUT OF THIS BOOK

I would recommend you try to read this book over a defined period, say between one and three months, and see it as a personal commitment to improving your communication skills. The more you consciously engage with the lessons and apply them to your life, the faster you will achieve mastery and become a more powerful communicator.

You can read it cover to cover, or cherry pick the chapters that are most suited to your needs at the time. Each chapter will stand alone, so dipping in and out will work well. You'll see that the chapters are divided into four main sections.

Part 1 supplies you with the tools and techniques that are essential to good communication.

Part 2 looks at that vitally important element – non-verbal communication – which is much more valuable than the actual words we say.

Part 3 is application-based and examines how to use the tools most efficiently in various specific situations, from interviews to speeches.

Part 4 goes in depth into the development of perfect enunciation and a powerful voice.

We learn by doing and by interacting. Therefore the more active the learning, the more The Communication Equation 3 your whole body will absorb the techniques. A great way to promote this absorption is by keeping a communication diary. This is simply a journal or a document on your computeror your phone in which you jot down your thoughts and experiences on the subject of communication while you are reading this book.

Journal exercise...

Every day, pick at least one item from the list below (if you have time, you could always do more than one) and write about it in your journal.

- Any examples you observed of good or bad communication.
- Any challenging communication situations you found yourself in. What you did well in that situation and what you could have done better.
- Did you use any techniques from Chapters 12 and 13 on defusing conflict?
- Any techniques you used from this book and how they worked for you.
- Any techniques you wished you'd used from the book, and what you imagine could have happened differently.
- Any interesting situations that occurred – what happened, what you did, how other people reacted, the outcome, and what, if anything, you could have done better.
- Read through your journal every week or fortnight to consolidate your learning.

LSW Gem: Stages of learning (II)

If you really want to make tangible changes to your communication skills, the four stages of learning offer a useful measure of your progress towards being a great communicator.

1. Unconscious incompetence

When you don't know what you don't know, you are powerless to change it. For example, if you mumble rather than talking clearly but don't realise it, you will never understand that there could be a better way of speaking.

2. Conscious incompetence

Let's say you get some feedback at work, perhaps your boss says that you're great but for your communication skills, which aren't up to scratch, as people can't understand you. This is where you become aware of an area that isn't working, but don't know what to do about it. It's at this stage that you are likely to pick up this book.

3. Conscious competence

Once you have read and engaged with the Serlin Method™, you start to move between stages two and three. You now understand what you are doing that isn't working, and you have learned how to stop mumbling and speak in a clear way. Both you and your colleagues are noticing changes. It's exciting. But it's also quite draining because you have to be so conscious of it all the time!

4. Unconscious competence

Finally, with some focused hard work and a whole lot of practice, you move from being a mumbler into the final stage. You have learnt the skill, it's gone deep into your muscle memory, and now when you open your mouth, the words come out with clarity and conviction, and you no longer need to think consciously about it. You decide – now that you have cracked communica-tion – to learn the piano. And off you go on the learning cycle once again.

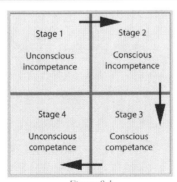

Figure 0.1
Stages of learning

As you complete the exercises in this book, it's important to reward yourself and celebrate your progress. The human brain responds extremely well to encouragement. The 'carrot' is the intangible quality that gets us to push further and faster. So if you have worked hard, done some of the exercises and have a sense that you have truly learnt something, then stop and celebrate!

By doing this, you are giving your brain a positive encouragement to take on the new learning, thereby treading in those new neural pathways even deeper and associating them with positive feelings so that you want to learn even more.

In order to properly engage with this book, you'll benefit if you:

1.   Do the exercises.

2.   Practise using a voice recorder and/or film yourself.

3.   Keep a communication diary.

DISCLAIMER: LIFE COULD START HAPPENING

I am working on a new idea for my company. Let's say I arrange a meeting with my boss in two weeks' time to tell him about it. And let's say, day three, someone gives me this book. I start to read. I practise the techniques. I engage with the principles. I rewrite the speech so it really gets to the heart of what I believe. I learn to deliver with my facial expression and engage with my voice and articulate with my body. I'm ready to go. And what happens? Possibly the worst thing, possibly the best. My delivery is exceptional. And it has more impact because they didn't see it coming. Quiet, solid, reliable me.

They never suspected I had so much passion in me. They give me the budget I ask for, ask me to pick my team, and report to my boss fortnightly to maintain his involvement with the entire operation. They love it. Life has started to happen. If you have good communication skills, you can inspire yourself and those around you. Life starts moving. Other people see your energy and it stimulates their energy, too. Watch out if you want to be just okay, because there's a chance you'll be heading for brilliant. Ask yourself: are you ready to be heard?

If you are, read on…

PART 1

The fundamental tools of communication

Chapter 1 | What makes an outstanding communicator? |

In this chapter you will learn about:

- **Physical clues:** And the assumptions we draw from them
- **Vocal landscape:** Creating an interesting backdrop
- **Core principles:** Five tenets of good communication
- **Social performance:** And why it is necessary in a great communicator's toolbox

Great communication is not about sounding perfect. It's about communicating to others in a way that makes them feel and think and want to take action. Whether the goal is to make someone feel interested or inspired, amused or motivated, the main point is to effect change in another person.

WE ALL KNOW WHAT IT'S LIKE to listen to someone who is a good communicator. Somehow they can make anything sound interesting; they can hold the attention of a crowd and bring people round to their way of thinking. One only needs to think of the great orators of past and present decades – Martin Luther King, Mahatma Gandhi, Susan B Anthony, Barack Obama, Brené Brown – to see evidence of this.

This chapter will explore some broad ideas of what makes a communicator great in order to set up the foundations of the rest of the book. It works through the physical clues we get from a communicator (the assumptions we make), through to the vocal ones (vocal landscape) through to five principal attributes that all great communicators have in common, finishing up with the need to step up a gear, or socially perform when the stakes or situation demand it.

Physical Clues

Before someone even opens their mouth, we have formed an idea of whether or not they will be a good communicator. Based on a range of physical clues, we form ideas about the speaker even without thinking about it: how much they care, their confidence levels, their passions and motivations. This is because we take shortcuts that help us to make these speedy assumptions about people.One shortcut we are particularly good at is reading people's physiology.

This isn't something most of us do consciously, it just happens. However, when we become conscious of exactly what we are reading, we can apply that knowledge to ourselves and take control of the impression we are making ourselves.

Discovering assumptions exercise...

To start, look at these two pictures:

Figure 1.1   *Figure 1.2*

Looking at these photos, you will probably agree that if you had to choose which person to listen to at a conference, you would veer towards the man in the first image.

Assumptions

Get ready to jot down some numbers in your communication diary (or you can fill in the box below). With 1 representing 0% and 10 representing 100%, score each speaker under the various headings listed below. What I want you to notice is how many assumptions we make with purely physiological information.

Your assumptions	Speaker 1	Speaker 2
How much do you want to listen to this person?		
How confident do you think they are?		

Do they care about what they are saying?		
How much do they care about you, their audience?		
How good do you imagine you will feel listening to them?		
How positive do you think their current mood is?		

Now total the two boxes and look at the score.

A high score means we believe that person will be a good communicator, even before we have heard them speak. A low score means the opposite. I expect most readers' numbers will reflect the same discovery: we have more positive beliefs about speaker 1 than speaker 2. By simply analysing someone's physiology we can build a good picture of whether we want to listen to them.

Feature descriptions

Now let's look at what we actually see. Again for each speaker, choose the most appropriate words and put them in the relevant box.

Feature	Description	Speaker 1	Speaker 2
Eyes	Disengaged, alive, vacant, engaged,bright, sagging		
Direction of gaze	Outwards, inwards, upwards, downwards, clear eye contact		
Direction ofattention	Outwards, inwards, upwards, downwards		
Posture orshoulder position	Sagging, hunched, closed, open, erect, shoulders back		
Use of hands orgestures	Sagging, hunched, closed, open, erect, shoulders back		

Again we are most likely to find that the box for speaker 1 has positive, active, energised words and for speaker 2 they are duller more inward-looking words. This gives us a broad picture of how and why we made these instinctive assumptions in the first place. We can then use this knowledge both for our own communication and to better assess the communication of others.

Here is my analysis:

Feature	Speaker 1	Speaker 2
Eyes	Bright	Dull
Direction of gaze	Clear eye contact	Downwards
Direction of attention	Outwards	Inwards
Posture or shoulder position	Erect	Sagging
Use of hands or gestures	Active, stretching to fingertips	Passive

That's from one picture – imagine what we could do with a whole 30 seconds looking at the actual person!

Assumptions we make about someone are actually based on simple things that we can all control. In other words, while it may be true that some people have a head start in their ability to communicate well, everyone has the power to make a positive impression if they learn the simple techniques. This book is going to give you the tools, techniques and awareness you can employ to change your communication skills and enable you to give the best possible impression.

Where to find out more:

Chapter 7 – How to use your body for effect

Chapter 8 – Facial expression to influence and captivate

Vocal Landscape

So now we have a sense of the importance of making the right physical impression. The next thing that happens is when the individual opens their mouth. Their tone of voice, the way they handle their words, the colour they inject into their sentences, their pauses, pace and emphasis, all of this builds a landscape in their listeners' minds.

In fact, this metaphor of a landscape is a particularly useful one for communication, and one that we use at LSW all the time. We call it the vocal landscape. This posits that the way in which you speak creates a vocal landscape for your listener, which can be boring or fascinating, depending on how you use your voice.

A great communicator will create a vocal landscape that is filled with colour, dimension and texture. Then they will direct their listeners' attention to the big ideas using their intonation and emphasis and, in doing so, engage and interest them. A weaker communicator will create a dull, barren, monochrome vocal landscape and, as a result, will struggle to hold their listeners' attention.

There are two brilliant things about creating an interesting vocal landscape: not only does it make what you are saying engaging for your listeners, but it also allows you to transmit your ideas – as you want them to be transmitted – into your listeners' minds. You are using your voice and the way you are speaking to indicate which words and ideas really matter.

In communication terms, this is quite effective: by putting energy into the vocal landscape, the speaker is able to have a certain power over the image created in their listeners' minds. It fast-tracks the communication process.

Look at the two pictures below. Imagine you were told to go sit in the middle of one of them for two hours. Which one would you choose?

Figure 1.3
Landscape 1

Figure 1.4
Landscape 2

Most of us have been in lectures where the speaker is so awful that, try as we might, we can't hold on to a single word or phrase – it's as though our brains are suddenly like an icy slope and everything just slithers off. They speak in a monotone with no variation of pace or volume. It's unnervingly similar to the barren landscape!

If no words or ideas have any emphasis or colour, then the speaker is giving no indication of which ideas are important or which words really matter in the speech. It's as if they are handing over a pile of words to their audience for them to construct the message for themselves.

On the other hand, we have all heard speeches which make our pulses race and imagination flow, as if the words are mainlining straight into us. This is an example of a great vocal landscape, which provokes the listeners' feelings and gives them space to come up with their own opinions and responses.

There are three components to creating an interesting vocal landscape:

1. **Word power** – the building blocks of words themselves, consisting of vowels and consonants.

2. **How you say what you say** – pace, emphasis, volume and intonation.

3. **Vocal expression** – colour and vocal range.

Where to find out more:

Chapter 2 – How words work
Chapter 4 – Delivering your message to its intended destination
Chapter 18 – Unleash your powerful voice

Core Principles

We believe there are five principles to being a great communicator. These are adapted from the seven Bushido virtues of the Samurai warrior.

- Authenticity corresponds with Makoto (honesty and sincerity).
- Courage corresponds with Yu (heroic courage).
- Connection corresponds to Jin (compassion).
- Commitment corresponds with Rei and Chu (respect and duty and loyalty).
- Purpose corresponds to Meiyo and Gi (honour and integrity).

義	礼	勇	誉	仁	真	忠義
GI	REI	YU	MEIYO	JIN	MAKOTO	CHU

Figure 1.5

Bushido virtues

When all the principles have a place in communication, then the communication can be transformative, it can touch people's hearts and minds, call them to act, inspire them to change, and the world can spin a little on its axis as a result.

Authenticity: This is about finding your connection with your message; being you and expressing yourself, not just in your words but with your voice and body language.

Courage: Daring to share your message, to reveal yourself, your passions and values. Daring to be seen. Daring to feel the fear and do it anyway.

Connection: Connecting to your audience so they feel important. The message has to be for them.

Commitment: Committing to sharing your ideas in a way that will do you and your message justice.

Purpose: Bringing an awareness of your purpose into your speech to align it with moral values that people respond to.

PRINCIPLE ONE: A GREAT COMMUNICATOR WILL BE AUTHENTIC

When you do things from your soul, you feel a river moving in you, a joy.

Rumi

The first principle of good communication is authenticity. If this were bread-making, authenticity is the yeast. Authenticity in communication is about two key ideas. The first is genuinely caring about what you are saying, enough to want to share those ideas with other people. The second is to make sure your listeners know that you care.

Caring about your message

If you don't care about your message, why should anyone else? You have to have a real desire to speak and, in order to do that, it helps to know why these words are important to you or how they resonate with you as a person. This concept of our message resonating with us on a personal level may seem a little unnecessary, particularly if it's a work presentation, but the more authenticity we get into any communication, the better it is, so it's worth doing well. Another way in can be to find the values that are important to you and then look at where your values and your message meet. This doesn't mean that everything we say has to be hugely important or serious, but more that to make it worth saying, it needs to strike a chord within us. Look at the section on values if you want to explore this further (see Chapter 10).

Showing others that you care

Sometimes you may feel authentic and wonder why it's not coming across. Well, pressure, fear, bad habits and lack of knowledge have a canny knack of getting in the way – particularly when the stakes are high! So once you have an authentic connection to your message, it is important to show your listeners you care, as otherwise you won't appear authentic. You can learn to overcome fears and break bad habits through using the tools in this book, using your voice, body and words, so that every element of you is coming together to share your message. It's so important that we know how to override the fears and show our true feelings about something because that is what makes a speech sing.

Authenticity top tip: Find where you and your message meet by deciding which words and sentences in your prepared text are most important to you.

Where to find out more:

Chapter 3 – Techniques to sound compelling
Chapter 5 – Overcoming nerves
Chapter 7 – How to use your body for effect
Chapter 8 – Facial expression to influence and captivate
Chapter 10 – Find out what makes you tick
Chapter 18 – Unleash your powerful voice

PRINCIPLE TWO: A GREAT COMMUNICATOR WILL BE COURAGEOUS

I want to sing like the birds sing, not worrying about who hears or what they think

Rumi

Courage is about two main things: taking action even when you feel fearful and being prepared to be vulnerable to your listener or audience.

Taking action when you feel fearful

To communicate powerfully, your desire to speak must be bigger than your fears. This means that your drive to be heard will give you strength to stand up to the demons of fear in your head, acknowledge them and say, 'Yes I may be scared, but I'll do it anyway.' And then if you stutter a little, if you wobble or sweat or pace the floor, it won't matter. Because you are daring to be bigger than your fear and you are courageous enough to share your real emotions.

Being prepared to be vulnerable

Courage is about being prepared to be vulnerable because what is driving you – your values, goals and vision – is so much bigger and more important than anything that is holding you back.

Vulnerability (in manageable doses) is good because it's real. And real stuff, particularly in business, is intoxicating. This isn't about crying in front of people or revealing your deepest secrets, it's about getting yourself involved so people feel you genuinely care about what you are saying. If you do that, they will want to get involved, too. When we dare to be vulnerable, we can really move people. It's a very powerful place to be.

The opposite of courage is staying safe

We all know people who stay safe in all contexts, keeping their feelings, passion and enthusiasm out of the picture. They do it because it's scary to step out of their comfort zone, and being in control is a much safer place to be. That works in many situations, but it will be a struggle to be a great communicator without revealing some of who you really are. I am not advocating flinging yourself out of the neat parameters of your safe space. But opening a window and letting in some fresh air could be a fantastic first step. A little bit of honest revelation, especially from someone who doesn't do it very much, can be incredibly moving.

Courage top tip: Consciously decide why speaking is more important to you than staying safe, and let that drive you forward if you waver.

Where to find out more:

PRINCIPLE THREE: A GREAT COMMUNICATOR BUILDS CONNECTIONS

Be grateful for whoever comes, because each has been sent as a guide from beyond.

Rumi

Connection is that magic moment between human beings when there is a meeting of hearts and minds. It transcends culture, language, age... everything. If you are skilled at building connections with others, then you will benefit from it throughout your life. Connection is where you reach out to your audience and make them feel important. Without it, you can communicate well, but never exceptionally well, because that requires people to feel changed as a result of what you have said.

Connection is about two components. The first is about delivering your message to your audience so that they know it is for them. The second is about listening and responding to your audience in a way that leaves them in no doubt as to their importance to you.

Delivering your message

Delivering your message is about speaking with intention and making sure that your ideas land at their intended destination. It's a simple idea, but bizarrely, one that so many speakers miss – particularly if they are reading from a piece of paper! Often their notes get the force of their meaning as they look down too much. It is crucial when communicating that your audience knows the story or speech is specifically for them, for if they don't, if they feel irrelevant in the communication dynamic, then why should they carry on listening?

Listening and responding

This is about tuning in to your audience and making sure that they feel they matter, about finding a genuine interest and listening in a deeper way than you might be used to. A great example of a speaker who built connections was Bill Clinton; we have a spotlight on him in the rapport section (see Chapter 9).

Connection is a great equaliser. It is not looking down from a great height but instead is reaching out to people, from one heart to the other. That's what great leaders have in common. That is also what Princess Diana did so well, earning her the title of 'the people's princess'.

Connection top tip: Deliver your ideas by looking at your audience in the final few words of each thought (typically before a full stop).

Where to find out more:

Chapter 3 – Techniques to sound compelling
Chapter 6 – The magic of connection spaces
Chapter 8 – Facial expression to influence and captivate
Chapter 9 – The true art of listening

PRINCIPLE FOUR: A GREAT COMMUNICATOR WILL COMMIT

Don't be satisfied with stories, how things have gone with others.
Unfold your own myth.

Rumi

To be a great communicator, you need to have a powerful reason for speaking and you need to be prepared to commit. Everyone who has a voice has a right to speak and be heard. But not everyone takes ownership of that right. There are people with louder voices who will try to drown out voices they don't want to hear. This principle is about committing to articulating your passion and about honouring your right to speak.

Your right to speak

This is not about speaking aggressively or forcing your opinion on others. But it is about committing to your right to speak, to your passion, and the fact that, if you wish it, your passion can have a voice. Nothing should get in the way of that. Of course, you can't force someone to listen, and if you don't speak in a way that makes people want to listen, then that is another issue. However, in the free world, your right to speak what is true to you is implicit. You have a voice, and no one gets to bully you out of communication unless you let them. This is a large point, because it is easy to come up with excuses – I'll get fired, they'll shout me down, I'll be punished – but none of those reasons has stopped other speakers with an intense desire to speak their mind. This principle is also one that many great films use as their basis: the underdog who finds his voice. Whatever the situation, there are times in life where every individual needs to say what matters to them, and claim their right to speak.

So if you feel circumstances have taken away your ability to speak your mind, then you can use the tools in this book to help you find it. From finding your vocal impact to helping you make dominant people more receptive to you, use this book to give you back your voice.

Commitment top tip: Freedom of speech is as relevant in day-to-day communication as anywhere else. Don't let yourself be bullied or intimidated out of telling others what you believe.

Where to find out more:

Chapter 5 – Overcoming nerves
Chapter 6 – The magic of connection spaces
Chapter 7 – How to use your body for effect
Chapter 10 – Find out what makes you tick
Chapter 13 – How to calm an angry person
Chapter 18 – Unleash your powerful voice

PRINCIPLE FIVE: A GREAT COMMUNICATOR WILL HAVE INTEGRITY

Let the beauty of what you love be what you do. There are a thousand ways
to kneel and kiss the earth.

Rumi

Integrity is about connecting to higher standards and ideals. When we work with themes that are bigger than us, we plug into a collective energy where what we are saying can resonate with the thoughts and passions of others. Through this we can catch and ride a wave of human emotion. To communicate with integrity is to bring your values and purpose to your speech. It is about the drive to speak holding you strong amidst all the things that could sway you off balance. If you are giving a speech with integrity, then your passion and commitment to your message will be measured against higher ideals that matter for others, not just for you.

Don't compromise your values

Integrity is lost if you are trying too hard to please your audience, compromising your values, in order to give them what they want. This is one of the big reasons why politicians – who so often change their tune in order to say what they think the electorate wants to hear – are thought of as duplicitous and lacking in integrity.

If you believe in what you are saying, it will have an effect on your body and your voice. Your spine will be erect. You will be instinctively connecting with the audience. You will have courage, commitment and be authentic.

Integrity top tip: Integrity is often about checking in with an inner guidance system, our own moral compass.

Where to find out more:

Chapter 7 – How to use your body for effect
Chapter 8 – Facial expression to influence and captivate
Chapter 10 – Find out what makes you tick
Chapter 16 – Delivering inspiring public speeches
Chapter 18 – Unleash your powerful voice

Social Performance

A useful idea to engage with at the start of this book is that of social performance. To meet the needs of a situation, we might need to perform a little or, to use another analogy, step up a gear. In general we communicate at a level that is comfortable for us. Some people might be naturally quite quiet and have a more subdued communication style so – to continue the gear analogy – they'd be in first gear. Others might be very boisterous in their day-to-day speech and be in fourth or fifth gear. Wherever we are at naturally may well be appropriate for most situations but occasionally we need to move up a gear.

While this notching up the gears may feel different from normal, it can still be authentic. Social performance is simply about committing to what needs to be done to get your message across in the most effective way. You can still be authentic at the same time as being bigger, louder and brighter than you might be in another situation.

WHEN WE SOCIALLY PERFORM

The need for social performance can come in all shapes and sizes, be it a presentation, a pitch, a wedding speech, or even just having a bad day at the office and having to pretend everything is okay. Often social performance is as much a part of your job as replying to emails. We don't expect you to be putting on a mini show every day. However, you need instant access to gear four or five when occasion demands it. Sometimes you may not feel in a very gear-five kind of mood, but it's about applying the tools and getting on with it.

Given that it's a very human instinct in the world of work to wear different hats in different circumstances, it is fortunate that our brains are set up in such a way to respond to our body's messages, irrespective of whether we are performing or having a genuine experience. If we are in a gear four or five mode – whether we really feel great or we are putting on a show – our bodies will start releasing endorphins that actually make us feel larger and more confident.

THE DIFFERENCE BETWEEN ACTING AND PERFORMING

Sometimes clients are concerned about feeling fake or coming across as insincere. They worry if they do something to their voice, that it will be like acting. But it's important to remember that there is a difference between acting and performing. Acting is when you are putting on a character, taking on a role that isn't you. Performing is when you are adding dimensions to your communication in order to achieve your communication goals. And as it's performing and not acting, it doesn't need to feel fake, just slightly bigger and more colourful than your usual level. In making changes and taking on new tools, it's going to feel different. But remember, 'different' is not fake.

What makes an outstanding communicator?
/ GOLDEN RULES /

1. A first impression is based on physical clues before a person even opens their mouth. We do this intuitively and yet we can easily make it conscious.

2. When we become aware of what prompts those assumptions, we can turn that awareness inwards and adjust our posture, facial expression, energy and delivery to give a good impression.

3. You can learn to create an interesting vocal landscape to give you power over the way your ideas are formed in a person's mind.

4. The five principles of great communication are there to support you when you are making an important speech or presentation.

5. It's useful to be prepared to perform when occasion demands it, which means notching up your delivery a gear while remaining true to yourself.

Chapter 2 | How words work |

In this chapter you will learn about:

- **Word power:** Understanding the power of a single word
- **Vowels: And** how they express our feelings
- **Consonants:** And their important role when we speak

The unique LSW approach begins by focusing attention on the foundations of good communication – words and the sounds that make up words – because our experience shows that if you engage with the sound, the word can become even more powerful. Drilling down into this concept, we explore the relationship between vowels and emotion, and how consonants fulfil their role in containing the emotion of the vowel. Finally, we look at some of the pitfalls of regional vowel sounds and dropped consonants, and demonstrate how to overcome them.

WORDS ARE PACKED WITH MEANING. They are little bundles of sounds that help us to transmit the subtleties of our ideas, thoughts and feelings to others. They have the potential to be incredibly powerful tools if used correctly. As with most things, if not used correctly they can be pretty redundant. This chapter is about getting the right attitude to words themselves – looking at how to engage with the vowels and how to articulate the consonants so that you can release the full potential of the word.

Word Power

To begin with word power is to begin with a celebration of words themselves. I love words. I love the fact that they can sound like what they're describing. This concept of words sounding like their meaning – called onomatopoeia – has been explored by psychologists and marketing experts alike, all curious to know how to manipulate this relationship. For us, the fact that the sound of the word can link to its meaning builds an awareness of the importance of the sound of the word and how it can help you release more meaning. To begin, let's take a look at the kiki bouba experiment. Look at the two shapes below. Which is kiki and which is bouba?

Figure 2.1
Kiki and bouba

It's a no brainer, right? The sharp shape is kiki. Say it and feel it slice through your mouth with its harsh 'k' sound. It's easy to associate 'kiki' with the idea of sarcasm or a sharp wit. But can you imagine if you were told kiki meant 'to connect warmly or compassionately'? It would feel wrong.

On the other hand, bouba could easily mean warm or compassionate. Because of its component sounds we associate it with soft or bubbly, warm and round. Why? Because the 'b' sound is a gentle pressing and rolling of the lips, and the long vowel 'ooh' gives plenty of room for human feeling.

Do you see? Words can release meaning through their sound if we engage with them fully. We don't need to understand a speaker's words to have a sense of their meaning. It shows us we can use every component of our speech – the sounds, the vowels – to create the sensation we want the listener to experience.

SHAKESPEARE, SOUNDS AND EMOTIONS

Of many writers who have explored this concept, Shakespeare understood and demonstrated it brilliantly. Shakespeare was a composer of human emotions, creating great emotional symphonies in his plays. Yet his instruments were not limited to words, storylines and characters; they were also sounds. If there are harsh consonants in the speech of a particular character, that will tell you something of their state of mind. If they have long vowels and soft consonants, it will imply they are in a calmer, softer place.

DID YOU KNOW?

The power of 'oh'

Hamlet says 'oh' more often than any other character in Shakespeare. 'Oh' – if you really engage with it, if you say it until your breath runs out – can be like a long drawn-out cry. Say it to yourself now, slowly over about 3 seconds (notice the same sound is in slowly, too) and see if you feel anything.

'Oh what a rogue and peasant slave am I.'

Hamlet's famous line from his soliloquy – filled with long vowels in 'oh', 'rogue', 'slave', 'I' – means that it is packed with emotion (long vowels provide opportunity for more emotion, as you will see as we learn more about vowels). The crisp 't' and 'p' of 'peasant' show a self-disgust, while the long vowels show a kind of mawkish despair, an emotional self-pity. Finally, the 'oh 'and 'I' bookend his pain with open vowels, with no consonants to contain the emotion spilling out from this line.

If you read a Shakespeare play or monologue with an awareness of the sounds used, engaging with the length of the vowels and the softness or hardness of the consonants, you can find yourself taken on the emotional journey that Shakespeare carved out for you all those centuries ago.

Vowels

Next we break words into their tiniest parts in order to understand how the building blocks of a word can be used to create impact.

So much of good communication in English is about the vowels. This is because vowels offer a space and time to fill with expression. If a speaker doesn't use their vowels to transmit feeling, then they will struggle to share their feelings with their listeners. And anyone listening to an emotionless speaker will struggle to stay focused.

This may seem quite a bizarre thought, but think about it. Emotions have to be shared through something: partly through your non-verbal communication – and we will come to that later in this book – and partly through the words that you choose. But neither of these tells us about expression or tone of voice, and that has to go somewhere. So emotions are shared mostly in vowels mainly because they are all made with an open mouth, and as such, the sounds have the advantage of taking some time and coming from inside of you.

Consonants, on the other hand, are a fleeting moment of contact between two parts of your mouth, so literally don't provide the time to share emotions.

Think of babies. When they are born they only make vowel sounds, in an array of cries which often only their mother can distinguish. The sounds they make come straight from inside and they are pure emotion. There is no thought or analysis that goes on, it's just simple needs, emotions and appetites, straight from the gut. Then as they grow and learn to form words, they learn to use consonants to contain that emotion.

That's why a word can be so powerful: it is a synthesis of control and efficiency, emotion and feeling.

DID YOU KNOW?

A telling ratio

In neutral spoken English, there are three types of vowel sound: short, long and diphthongs. Diphthongs are a mixture of two vowels put together so are extra long. You don't need to remember the name – but some of the numbers are interesting. There are 20 vowel sounds in total. Out of the 20, 7 are short. That leaves 13 vowels that are long or, in the case of diphthongs, even longer.

More room, therefore, for layer upon layer of feelings to inspire, engage and motivate your listeners or audience. That gives a clue as to why the English language, and the classic, neutral English accent, has such popularity on a global scale. It allows so much room for emotional connection.

SHAKESPEARE, VOWELS AND INFLUENCE

Once you think of the vowels as containing the emotion of the word, you can begin to understand where actors get their power from. For a great example of this, look for 'Henry V – St Crispin's Speech' by William Shakespeare on YouTube, where you can find Kenneth Brannagh starring in Shakespeare's *Henry V*, performing the St Crispin's Day speech (Act IV, Scene iii).

The speech is filled with long vowel sounds which Brannagh uses to pour emotion into his words. In the speech, he incites his men to fight to the death, despite being outnumbered three to one. When the men cheer and charge, inspired and motivated despite the odds against them, we are not surprised. In fact, it's easy to imagine joining in. And that, quite simply, is the power of language, and transmitting feeling and meaning through words and sounds. It's based on a true story and, as it happens, the English did beat the French despite the odds. If a speech is so powerful it incites men to go willingly into a battle when death is almost inevitable, then it is going to be filled with emotion. And Shakespeare knew that the best way to transmit emotion is through long vowels.

I have taken an extract of the speech and highlighted the diphthongs and long vowels, so you can see for yourself. Shakespeare knew what he was doing!

*This **day** is call'd the **feast** of Crispian.*

*He that **out**lives this **day**, and comes **safe** home,*

*Will **stand** a tip-**toe** when this **day** is nam'd,*

*And **rou**se him at the **name** of Crispian.*

LSW Gem: Use vowels for time control

Long vowels can act as an anchoring point when you are speaking. They can slow you down, give you back control, give you time to check the effect of your words on your audience. Long vowels give you the option to drag out a thought — take perhaps 10 seconds saying a line rather than three. This allows you to subtly control time, making implicit statements to the person you are speaking to: I have your time in my hands; I have plenty of time. If you are stretching out the vowels, you can't be interrupted because you have not yet arrived at the end of the word.

The clichéd sounds of the British aristocracy involve very long vowels, and the theory fits well here. They not only had more time, they were in control of other people's time, so by lengthening their sounds, they were asserting status. The working classes — back, let's say, 100 or so years ago — typically had a shorter, more functional set of vowels, again consistent with their relationship to time.

VOWELS AND EMOTIONAL RELEASE

Making vowel sounds involves shifting the position of the tongue and the shape of the mouth in order to shape the sound. But essentially, all vowels are made with an open mouth, and if we don't open our mouths when we speak, then it's very difficult to let out any emotion. If we hold our feelings in, not expressing them by making our vowels short, monotone or keeping our mouths closed, then our feelings are either forced to come out elsewhere, through gesture and body language, or are suppressed.

To divert emotion through body language rather than expressing it through vowels is quite common with non-native speakers, who have a lot of energy but don't know how to channel it effectively through their speech, so it comes out through strong gestures. When we work with these clients on redirecting their energy into their vowels, their spoken communication is transformed.

Pushing down emotion is more endemic in native English speakers, and can be connected to the clichéd English characteristic of restraint.

However, if we don't use our vowels effectively to release our emotions in our speech, then we can struggle to connect. It can also be unhealthy as there is no emotional outlet. This link between vowels and feeling shows us that how we express ourselves in the world is linked to how we feel. And this is not just psychological but physiological, too.

You might find that by doing things, such as opening your mouth more when you speak, you feel different, perhaps vulnerable or exposed, or as though you are stepping out of your comfort zone and allowing yourself to be seen in a way you haven't been seen before. You can demonstrate it for yourself in the following exercise.

Engaging with vowels exercise ...

Say this line in two different ways:

'I want to go home'.

The first time, try saying the word 'home' as speedily as possible. The second time, try keeping your mouth open for longer while you say it, really elongating the 'oh' sound. Hear the difference? Feel the difference? In the second one, although it might sound silly, in that 'oh' of home, all sorts of longing can be expressed. 'She must be really missing home!' In fact, we can start to tell a story about the speaker.

Just by engaging with one word, we can release all sorts of meaning for the listener. This is why actors (who spend years training their voices and learning to engage with text) can be so successful at making the audience feel different emotions.

Case study: Don't incarcerate your vowels

I once had a client who came to me wanting to be rid of faint tones of a Swiss accent audible through his almost-perfect English. He spoke three languages, was highly intelligent and articulate and barely opened his mouth when he spoke. He came wanting accent-softening, but soon found himself in the pithy world of effective communication.

In an early session, I was working with him to use his vowels and I told him they were, in essence, the soul of the word. When he listened to a recording of his own speech, he realised how little he opened his mouth, and he said one of the most eloquent statements about vowels I've heard. He said the whole of his life he had been incarcerating his vowels in the words, as if he had locked their souls behind bars.

If we don't properly use the sounds of the words, we risk incarcerating their meaning. This means that our powers to influence and engage as a communicator are stunted from the moment we open (or in some cases barely open) our mouths.

Consonants

There are two reasons to accurately pronounce consonants. The first is that consonants balance and contain the emotion of the vowel. The second is that if some consonants are dropped or muddled, this makes an implicit statement about our relationship with the language and can also place us in a particular location or social group. Whether you like it or not, you may think it is worth having the tools at your fingertips to be able to adapt your accent if you wish to. Would Ian McKellen be as distinguished and popular an actor if he spoke only with a broad Lancashire accent?

CONSONANTS CONTAIN THE VOWEL

While vowels hold the emotional content of what we are saying, consonants have a very different role in the psychology of English speech. They contain the emotion of the vowel, representing accuracy, efficiency and, in a strange way, respect for the language.

Together, then, vowels and consonants make up the perfect English character: emotional and romantic, yet contained and proper. For while we English are filled with emotion, we also like to be in control, especially of our emotions.

Within our vocal landscape, consonants are the firm edges. They provide definition to our ideas; they stop the objects in the environment from merging into each other. If we leave them out, ideas can merge into other ideas, leading to a lack of clarity.

For me, the importance of accurate pronunciation of consonants is less about bowing to the social system and more about valuing language and the power of fully using the words to respect our ideas. Consonants provide definition to our ideas. In the vocal landscape you are constructing, consonants are the walls, the straight lines, the edges that hold the buildings in place.

CONSONANTS AND THEIR ROLE IN BRITISH SOCIETY

Like it or not, people make judgements when they hear words pronounced with missing or muddled consonants. Speakers may be judged in terms of class, education or even intelligence. That's a like-it-or-lump-it situation and, to be honest, I am not sure I like it. However, having the choice means that you have control over what people think of you, and that is a power that everyone aspiring to be a good communicator can benefit from.

Consonants can also represent respect for the word and the language itself. If I say a word and leave the consonant off the end, or if the consonants are absent or muddled, it can imply that the word is not that important to me, as I am not bothering to say it properly.

This is fine if that is how we feel about the language, and for many accents all over Britain, particularly in parts of London, there seems to be an implicit rebellion in a way of speaking which drops and switches consonants. There is nothing wrong with this, as long as it is what is intended.

CONSONANTS – A SHARP BLADE

Words can be thought of as powerful tools with sharp blades that can achieve very precise goals. If we blunt that tool and throw it, do we still expect it to hit with as much finesse and precision? Of course not.

Take the words 'hate' or 'smart', or 'sweet' or 'bitter'. If we want these words to have their full power we need to express them fully. Can you imagine the Samurai warrior waving around a bluntish sword? No! He uses his instruments well and with total precision.

It does not mean every word needs to be perfectly articulated to the letter. In fact, the English language actually requires you to connect words into a flow of language, losing a few consonants on the way.

So, there are only two situations where you really do need to accurately pronounce a consonant: at the end of an important word or thought (to contain it), and in between two vowels. For example, if I said, 'At the end of an important thought' and dropped the final T – it would sound sloppy. Similarly, if I said, 'It doesn't matter' and dropped the two Ts in the middle of the word 'matter', it would sound as though it didn't matter!

It's one thing to know that consonants are sharp blades, crucial to defining your ideas and delivering them with impact, and quite another to know how to use those blades, how to define your words effectively if you've got out of the habit. If you feel that you are prone to dropping or switching consonants, then read Chapter 17, You can learn beautiful enunciation, for some exercises to get you into shape.

How words work
/ GOLDEN RULES /

1. Remember the sounds of words can express their meanings so use them accordingly.

2. If you don't open your mouth very much, then it's very difficult to let any emotion out, and emotion is how we connect and inspire.

3. Vowels are a space for your feelings, so fill that space with some expression, not just sound.

4. Consonants contain the emotion of the vowel. They give it edge and definition.

5. You can drop some consonants and get away with it, but not in between a word or at the end of a thought.

Chapter 3 | Techniques to sound compelling |

> ## In this chapter you will learn about:
>
> - **Emphasis:** And how to use it to draw in the listener
> - **Pauses:** Using beats to divide up our thoughts
> - **Psychological hooks:** Devices that add colour to our words
> - **Pace:** Establishing a comfortable speed for you and your listener

Why is it that one person giving a presentation can sound like fingernails scraping down a blackboard, whereas another person is totally engaging, like spreading warm butter on toast? How do they do that? It is not magic. Quite simply, one person is making you work very hard whereas the other is doing all the work for you.

IN THIS CHAPTER we are going to look at four specific ways to sound compelling. Firstly, we look at emphasis, how to pick out important words that draw in the listener, and secondly, how to use pauses to divide up our thoughts and maintain control and interest. Then we'll give you some professional tips on a clever little tool we call psychological hooks, which will help you add colour to your words. Finally, we look at the importance of finding the right pace so that your listener feels at ease. If you are sitting up straight enough to connect with your diaphragm and are using these techniques, then people will listen. This stuff works.

The LSW intonation technique is one of our most powerful methods. There are three steps:

1. **Emphasis** - Pull out the important words in your speech.

2. **Pauses** - Speak in smaller units of information.

3. **Psychological hooks** - Put colour in your voice to keep your listeners attentive.

We'll look at each of these in turn.

Emphasis

We use emphasis to draw attention to the important words, but which words do we choose? To put it simply, there is a word hierarchy and not all words were born equal. There are words that hold information, and words that only facilitate information. This section is about which words are which.

The best communicators reflect this hierarchy with their voice, energy and breath, emphasising only those words that contain meaning while letting other words – the grammatical words – take a back seat. Why? In essence, English is an efficient language: its structure allows the speaker to do very little to achieve maximum effect, and what they do is direct energy only to specific places, namely the stressed syllable of the most important words.

This is often where non-native speakers get stuck. You can be as fluent as you like, but if you give each word equal weight, then you are sacrificing the melody and the full power of the English language. We can look at this more closely using the metaphor of a car.

THE CAR METAPHOR

There are two categories: front-seat words and back-seat words. We use emphasis to separate them into groups for the listener by signposting what is and is not important.

Front-Seat Words: These are words that hold information which adds to our understanding of the ideas or story. The difference between front-seat words, like 'cat' or 'running', and back-seat words like 'is' and 'there' is that when you hear a front-seat word you can usually picture it in some way, whereas a back-seat word holds little meaning out of context.

Back-Seat Words: These are the in-between bits-and-pieces words that are almost invisible in a conversation. They are grammatical noises that populate our sentences to make the meaning more sophisticated by signposting, for example, gender or tense. In themselves, they do not supply meaning. Examples are 'he', 'she', 'did', and so on.

Word hierarchy exercise...

This exercise is a powerful illustration of how some words contain meaning whereas others simply facilitate it.

1.   **Choose your words.**

2.   **Record yourself reading this excerpt.**

But peace does not rest in the charters and covenants alone. It lies in the hearts and minds of all people. So let us not rest all our hopes on parchment and paper, let us strive to build peace ... in the hearts and minds of all people.

(Excerpt from John F Kennedy's speech September 20, 1963 Address to the UN General Assembly)

Now look at the extract again and underline all the words you think are front-seat words. Don't worry if you are unsure, we have helped you out below.

3.   Now if we were to separate the underlined from the non-underlined, you should have two groups of words like this:

Group one: non-underlined words:

but, does, not, in, the, and, it, in, the, and, of, so, us, not, our, on, and, let, us, to, in, the, and, of.

Group two: underlined words:

peace, rest, charters, covenants, alone, lies, hearts, minds, all, people, rest, all, hopes, parchment, paper, strive, build, peace, hearts, minds, all, people.

Choose your images

Imagine you have a paint brush, some paints and a blank canvas in front of you. You are asked to draw a picture of the images that come to mind with the first group of non-underlined (back-seat) words. Then you are asked to draw a picture of what comes to mind with the second group of underlined words.

What does your canvas look like in group one – the non-underlined words?

And what does your canvas look like in group two – the <u>underlined</u> words? I imagine that the group one canvas will be like an abstract painting if anything, perhaps some marks or dashes on the paper, but no meaning at all. This collection of words could be said with all the expression in the world, but you still would struggle to paint anything of any substance or meaning.

In the second painting, there would be all kinds of objects and images. It may not be fully sophisticated or make perfect sense, but it is likely to be full of meaning and images.

Impose your emphasis

4.   Record the piece again, this time putting your emphasis on the information words. I have highlight   ed them in the text below.

TIP - Speed through the grammatical words quite quickly and use them simply as stepping stones to get to the information words.

> But **peace** does not **rest** in the **charters** and **covenants alone.** It **lies** in the **hearts** and **minds** of a**ll people.** So let us not **rest** all our **hopes** on **parchment** and **paper,** let us **strive** to **build peace ...** in the **hearts** and **minds** of **all people.**

5.   Listen back to the two recordings and ask yourself the following questions as if you were a third party:

•   Did the speaker care about what they were saying?

•   Did the speaker care about their listener?

•   Did you (the listener) care?

You should find a dramatic difference in the responses to these questions, from a negative response to the first recording to a positive one in the next.

LSW Gem: Longer, louder, higher

Emphasising a word is pretty instinctive for most of us, particularly when we are angry or passionate about something. However, some people wrongly assume that emphasis is simply speaking louder, and this can end up sounding aggressive.

As well as volume, we can emphasise our words by lingering a little longer on them, or by raising our pitch a bit higher. Essentially, any kind of vocal highlighting you do will achieve emphasis.

LSW Gem: Final word impact

Why is the final word of the thought or unit so important?

It's simple. Because of the way the English sentence is structured, the impact of the meaning of the sentence arrives on the final word. Look at the sentence below:

'An idea is nothing without its destination.'

If you remove the final word, the sentence doesn't mean anything.

'An idea is nothing without its.'

The thought makes full sense only when you get to the final word because it gives meaning to all that comes before it. So that is where you need to engage the audience. Don't let a final word sink without a trace, as that will undermine the value of the thought preceding it.

Pauses

Our working memory only has a certain amount of bandwidth. If we try to squeeze too many words into one breath, then the listener is unable to hold all of our ideas. This is what is happening when it becomes very difficult to follow someone. Their sentences are too long and they are packing too many words into one breath or unit. Using pauses or mini-beats as dividers is one of the most effective ways to share your ideas. We are not talking about long, empty pauses, but short beats which frame a unit of thought. This makes you sound steady and in control, which, in turn, helps the listener to process what you are saying and stay with you.

It is important to remember that unit breaks are not bound by punctuation, and even if we have a very long sentence, we can still communicate in such a way that helps the listener to follow our meaning by breaking up our thought into smaller chunks.

DID YOU KNOW?

The magic seven

'The Magical Number Seven, Plus or Minus Two: Some Limits on Our Capacity for Processing Information' (1956, George A Miller) is one of the most highly cited pieces of research on working memory. It revealed that the number of 'chunks' that a human can recall immediately after a presentation is between five and seven.

Keep in mind, then, that there is a finite amount that our working memories can absorb. The magic seven is therefore a very useful number to remember as seven words (or seven information words at a push) are just about as much as we can handle before we start to forget the first word of the sentence.

HOW TO ADD PAUSES

Adding pauses to a sentence is about dividing up our thoughts into mini-thoughts, with small beats or break points as we go, which usually fall between two and seven words. Read the following paragraph, which includes a beat on each /, and imagine that it is someone speaking to you. Notice how steady it feels.

These units of thought / make the listener feel comfortable / and give you, the speaker, / time to process as you go / and, where necessary, / make sure your mouth and tongue / are in the right place. By using units, / we can hold the hand of our listener, so to speak, / and take some thinking time, too. / This idea is at the very heart/ of being an engaging speaker.

This technique has so many advantages. You will never get tongue-tied or feel as if you are running ahead of yourself not knowing what to say next. You now have the time to connect with your listener and to think on your feet, and the time to engage with long vowels and inject some emotion into your words, which simply cannot be achieved if you talk at a high speed.

Pauses top tip: Unit breaks sit well after information words but not after grammatical words, as the grammatical words are useful to take you some-where.

Give me a break exercise...

Have a go with the text below, adding a line / where you think a break or beat could go. It tends to be intuitive and you can easily sense when to add a beat. First try saying the following sentences in one breath.

When we Americans first began, our biggest danger was clearly in view: we knew from the bitter experience with King George III that the most serious threat to democracy is usually the accumulation of too much power in the hands of an executive, whether he be a king or a president.

'Democracy Itself Is in Grave Danger', Al Gore

If you try to say this whole sentence in one breath, it leaves you very little energy to do anything interesting with it, like adding colour and tone, or emphasising certain words.

Now take a moment to put in unit breaks. Say it again and notice how different it feels and sounds.

THE £10 BREATH – RAISING THE VALUE OF YOUR WORDS

Remember that, when we speak, we are making an implicit statement about the value we place on our words.

Imagine each unit of speech is £10 in value. So every time you are breaking up a sentence into smaller units, you are increasing the overall value of the sentence. If you say a sentence without pausing, it is only worth £10. If you add, say, five pauses or unit breaks, it is worth £60. This corresponds with how much energy you are able to give it. If you are saying the whole sentence in one breath, you simply don't have the breath or energy to emphasise certain words. If, on the other hand, you have inserted pauses, you can give a lot more energy to each unit, thereby raising the overall value. In the moment when our energy, our breath and our intention meets our words and our ideas, we have the opportunity to make magic happen for our listeners.

LSW Gem: Multi-syllabled words

If I choose a multi-syllabled word because it is a better tool than a simpler word, I must take account of the fact that it demands more processing time from the listener, so it may even need a whole unit to itself in order to make a full impact. Otherwise it can easily become a word that passes over the listener's head as they try to make sense of the whole sentence. We can all remember times, in lectures or at conferences, when the words ceased to have any meaning. This would have been remedied if the speaker had given more energy to the multi-syllabled words.

So highlight your multi-syllabled words with your voice in order to ensure your speech makes its full impact. Look at the Al Gore speech in the exercise above. The word 'accumulation' is a classic example of a multi-syllabled word that could easily get lost if it is not given the time it needs.

Psychological Hooks

If we don't use our voice to demonstrate the logic of these units, it can sound as though we are stopping and starting for no reason. We do this by putting some colour in our voice over one particular word in each unit. We call this a psychological hook because it literally hooks the attention of your listener – like giving a tug on a puppy's lead every so often to make sure the puppy knows you are there.

One result of this is that you give the impression you are actively engaging with the words as you speak.

HOW IT WORKS

There is so much to attend to at any one moment that our brains select what is really worth attending to, and one way of making that judgement is by interpreting the tone of voice. If you speak in a dull monotone and seem bored by your own message, then the listener can justify switching off. But if someone's tone of voice reveals they believe something is amazing, they will tug on your lead and you will want to know about it!

Processing time: Psychological hooks can also buy you processing time if you are struggling to find your next word. You can do this by leaning into a word, and drawing out (lengthening) a vowel. If you are in a high-pressure meeting, for example, this is a fantastic way to buy time without getting flustered or stalling in the middle of your speech.

Variation: To make your psychological hooks effective you need to do something different with your tone in each unit. If you use exactly the same intonation, such as rising at the same point, it does not sound like you are engaged with what you are saying and it can easily sound robotic. Think about discovering each unit and showing its uniqueness with your voice.

Choosing your words: Always put hooks on front-seat words, never back-seat words, because they are the ones you want to draw attention to.

Intonation technique exercise...

You will need about 15 minutes and a recording device. Begin by recording yourself reading this extract:

All children, except one, grow up. They soon know that they will grow up and the way Wendy knew was this. One day she was playing in a garden when she plucked another flower and ran with it to her mother.

Step one:

Locate the information words. We have done it for you below. Record yourself putting emphasis into the highlighted words, really engaging with them and speeding through the grammatical words. Linger especially over the meaningful words.

All CHILDREN, except ONE, GROW UP. They soon KNOW that they will grow UP, and the WAY Wendy knew was THIS. One DAY, when she was TWO YEARS OLD, she was PLAYING in a Garden, and she PLUCKED another flower, and RAN with it to her MOTHER.

Step two:

Now we put in natural break points, as we have done below. I have also put capitals for where a psychological hook could be, so do something with your voice over these words. Have a practice run getting used to doing something new in each unit. Remember it is just a little beat.

Tip: You will find that the little bit of colour in your voice happens in the vowel sound of one or two of the important words. Often it will be the word at the end of the unit but, as you can see from the extract below, there is room for manoeuvre.

All CHILdren/ except ONE, /GROW UP./ They soon KNOW/ that they will grow UP, /and the WAY Wendy knew /was THIS./ One DAY, /when she was TWO YEARS OLD, /she was PLAYING in a Garden,/ and she PLUCKED another flower, /and RAN with it to her MOTHER.

Re-record

When you are ready, record yourself saying this piece again using pauses and psychological hooks. Enjoy making each unit interesting. Compare your final recording with the first one.

Do it yourself exercise...

Now do the same five steps with a text of your own or use the one below:

- – Record yourself reading the text
- – Put in emphasised words
- – Mark in pauses
- – Insert psychological hooks
- – Re-record the text

We meet this evening, not in sorrow, but in gladness of heart. The evacuation of Petersburg and Richmond, and the surrender of the principal insurgent army, give hope of a righteous and speedy peace whose joyous expression can not be restrained. In the midst of this, however, He from whom all blessings flow, must not be forgotten.

Final Public Address, Abraham Lincoln

Annotations and conclusions

When you listen to both recordings, imagine they are two different people speaking and ask yourself the following questions.

- - How does the speaker feel about what they are saying?
- - How does the speaker feel about you the listener?
- - How does listening to this piece make you feel?

Case study: Barack Obama

If you listen to a speaker like Barack Obama in his early campaign speeches, you will hear that they are made up of the tiniest units – often only two or three words. This worked for him on so many levels, raising the value of what he was saying. If we think back to the example of the £10 breath earlier in this chapter, each word was the equivalent of about £5 and therefore had plenty of human value. His subtext was, 'everything I say is of enormous value'.

We cannot get away with this kind of speaking most of the time, because it is only in certain circumstances that people would be willing to believe it; but an inauguration speech is one of them.

In many ways, Obama's election as president depended on people feeling as though he was walking with them. He came across as inspired, passionate and one of the people. In fact, his use of the collective pronoun 'we' was part of his entire slogan 'yes we can'. He understood better than anybody the importance of harnessing the power of the collective and making sure people were engaging with him on his journey. The way in which he spoke was a huge part of his success.

Pace

When we get nervous, we speed up. When we speed up, we can lose connection with our listeners, so it's vital to speak at the right pace.

We speak to get what's in our heads into other people's heads. Therefore we need to speak at a pace that makes it easy for them to absorb our thoughts, rather than at the pace of our own thoughts. This is not good communication, as we are giving our own thoughts priority.

In the same way you would adapt your walking pace to the person you are walking with, you adapt your speaking pace to the person you are speaking with. Imagine you are walking with a 90-year-old woman with a hip replacement; you slow down, right? Well, communicating is much the same because communication is a collaborative operation.

SLOWING DOWN

However, there is a world of difference between telling you to talk at the right pace and telling you to slow down. A speaker shouldn't be thinking about slowing down because they need to put their focus and energy into the speech. If they focus on slowing down rather than communication, it will lead to a sagging, under-energised style, like taking the hot air out of a balloon. Instead, use our LSW intonation technique (from the intonation technique exercise earlier in this chapter), which ensures that each word can be understood whilst the message remains full of colour and tone.

GETTING AWAY WITH SPEED

Sometimes people talk quickly and they get away with it. What about them? Talking quickly is not entirely out of the question all the time, but you have to earn your right to talk fast. To do this, you need to begin speaking with total clarity – no garbled consonants – and you have to hook your audience into the subject matter. By starting at a steady pace you are, in effect, calibrating your listener to your pace and energy, to the melody of your internal language. When this starts to happen, their energy and eye contact will be totally focused on you, their attention is your attention, and then you can speed up.

Judging pace exercise...

There is no 'correct' pace, but we all know when we are listening to someone who makes us feel either extreme. With the following text, let's experiment with four paces. Start with super-slow and work your way up to super-fast, then play around. Finally go to the pace where you felt most comfortable. When you are in the most comfortable pace, note if anything else changes.

- **Super-slow** – boring
- **Slow** – calm and guided
- **Fast** – energised
- **Super-fast** – rushed and frenetic

Fellow people in this here world: I stand before you tonight under indictment for the alleged crime of having voted at the last presidential election, without having a lawful right to vote. It shall be my work this evening to prove to you that me thus voting, I not only committed no crime, but, instead, simply exercised my citizen's rights, guaranteed to me and all United States citizens by the National Constitution, beyond the power of any state to deny.

On Women's Rights to Vote by Susan B. Anthony

Techniques to sound compelling
/GOLDEN RULES/

1. Words that hold information and meaning need to have more energy than grammatical words.

2. Make sure that you don't have too many words in a unit. Remember, that reduces the value you have given to your ideas.

3. Using pauses or unit breaks is a brilliant tactic for dealing with nerves and for buying yourself time in a pressured situation.

4. Add colour to your voice in information words in every unit to act as psychological hooks for your listener.

5. Communicate at a pace that works for your listener so you can take them with you on the journey.

Chapter 4 | Delivering your message to its intended destination |

In this chapter you will learn about:

- **The power of intention:** And how to harness it when communicating
- **Eye contact:** And how it should be done
- **Using your voice:** How to deliver your ideas effectively

We have explored emphasis, pausing and psychological hooks to bring phrasing and music into your speech. But giving an amazing speech to an audience of one hundred people is pointless if you have your back turned to them. Delivery is about making sure your communication goes all the way to its intended destination because if your ideas don't hit their mark, you might as well be singing your heart out to an empty room.

IT'S A LITTLE LIKE SENDING SOMETHING important via regular mail versus signed-for delivery. Regular mail is the equivalent of a quick glance at your audience – 'it's probably arrived' – while signed-for is paying extra and having proof that it arrived at its destination. That's what we do with things we value, so if we value our message, we must make sure it arrives safely at its destination.

Good delivery boils down to three main concepts. Firstly, intention; you must intend your message to reach your audience. Secondly, eye contact; using your eyes to make sure your idea has been delivered. Thirdly, vocal delivery; using your voice to deliver your message.

The Power of Intention

Intention is defined as an act or instance of determining mentally upon some action or result. We focus our energy on our intention so, when we are communicating, we need to intend to get our ideas to the listener. If we focus our attention elsewhere – thinking about whether we will be okay, if people will like us – we've lost the power of intention.

When we teach this concept at London Speech Workshop, we use a range of exercises to make sure our clients really understand when they have delivered an idea to the listener. It's the difference between talking at someone and communicating with someone. One of our favourite exercises is called spoons. It's a useful way to ensure the client feels the power of intention when it comes to delivery. It's also a useful metaphor to see the common mistakes that people make.

DELIVERY AND THE SPOON EXERCISE

Firstly, we give a client a bundle of spoons and a paragraph of text. Their task is to deliver a spoon with each unit from the text. Their coach won't take the spoon if it's not delivered, by which I mean the spoon has to be consciously placed in the coach's hand. It sounds simple, but it's not as easy as it sounds! Most people start off prioritising reading the text rather than connecting with their coach or delivering the spoon. It's only when they switch to making their primary intention placing the spoon in the hand that the magic starts to happen. As they realise their speed doesn't matter, they slow down and their words gain impact. Usually after about three spoons, there is a powerful 'aha' moment and the client starts to feel the connection they are making. Their speech becomes more powerful, and even though they are reading a text they

Delivering the spoon exercise...

1. Pick up a text.
2. Divide it into units.
3. Grab some random objects or a handful of things from your cutlery drawer.
4. Mark a spot as the 'hand' of your listener.
5. Pick up your text and deliver each unit with an item.

have never seen before, it starts to feel like it is theirs. Try it yourself.

COMMON MISTAKES

The spoon exercise demonstrates some of the common mistakes speakers make in their delivery.

The undelivered spoon

This is the person who simply puts each spoon down in front of their listener rather thanplacing it in their hand. They don't want to make a connection because it makes them uncomfortable. As a result, they create a wall between themselves and their listeners which the audience can look over. 'Oh look, he's twitching, he's nervous. He's scratching his neck.'

The good news is that all it requires is a few moments of delivery – intentionally placing your ideas with eye contact and energy into the audience – to grab your power back.

The spoon that's almost given, but taken back

This is the person who, despite having many of the qualities of a good speaker, doesn't quite manage to deliver their message to the audience. While they technically do a lot of the right things, they are missing the connection. They push out their words and then almost suck them back in at the end of each unit. So you get the feeling, listening to this person, that they are thinking about themselves rather than their audience. It is as if they are saying, 'I'm not really interested in you. In fact, I am more interested in me, and showing off with my next thought.' Some would say this particular trait is typical of most figures in British politics.

If this is you, you need to consciously use your voice and eyes to hit your message home to the audience that they are important. If you don't make them feel important, you are back to the empty-room analogy.

Forgotten spoons – the fade-out

Many speakers fade out on the final word of their sentence. Their volume and tone reduces as if they have run out of air or momentum. This is the equivalent of coming at the listener, full of energy, with a spoon, only to give up at the last minute and drop the spoon on the floor. At best, the listener feels ambivalent, at worst, disengaged. If the speaker can't be bothered to sustain interest in their thought, why on earth should the listener?

Again, you need to deliver with your voice, eyes and energy all the way through to the final word of your thought. If you are running out of air, speak in smaller units.

Giving spoons without care

This is the last of the common mistakes and the most unpleasant. This is when the speaker just holds out a spoon, not looking, expecting the listener to take it. It's the kind of speaking you could imagine a very regal, imperious type of person doing, like Judi Dench playing Elizabeth I in *Shakespeare in Love*. She'll throw her words out with no regard for her listener with the confidence that, because of her status, people will catch them. But we feel that it is alienating or even insulting to assume that the words are so important the speaker doesn't need to see if they have hit their target. People often do this when they are multi-tasking, particularly if they are doing something on a phone. The result is alienating listeners and not doing either task properly.

If this is you, re-evaluate your reason for speaking, the goals of your communication and how you want to make your listeners feel.

Eye Contact

The job of our eyes is not just to take in information. When we make eye contact with another human, there is no doubt that we are paying attention to each other. Eye contact is the most powerful way of demonstrating this connection between people, yet with no physical link between them. We all understand the cliché of eyes meeting across a crowded room. Two people know, in that moment, they are occupying a shared space in each other's minds. It's pretty powerful stuff.

Eyes can also express intention. Think of aiming a bow and arrow at a mark on a tree. Imagine looking at the point on the tree you hope to hit with your arrow, and the process of pulling your arm back. Just before you loose the arrow, can you feel what happens with your focus? There's a little increase in attention. The other noises and sights fade out. Now imagine trying to do it with your eyes closed. Not impossible, but difficult. A person who has no use of their eyes will learn to deliver with intention. But if you have full use of your eyes, this is the best place to start. Using your eyes to deliver an idea, with the same intent you would use to shoot an arrow, adds a huge power to your speech.

WHEN DO WE MAKE EYE CONTACT?

Effective eye contact is not about staring someone in the eye until they want to look away. It is about delivering a message and making sure it has been understood. To do this, it is only necessary to look at the audience during the final word or two of the sentence or important units. This is because that is where the impact of the message should be.

Remember we said that the final word makes sense of all that comes before and that without the final word, the sentence loses its meaning. This is why we need to deliver our idea on the final word or two of the thoughts or sentence.

Most people, if they are delivering a presentation from a text, will look up in the middle of their text and then look down at the end of their sentence to grab the next sentence. This gives the impression that they don't care about making sure their audience really gets their point.

This simple tool is so little known and yet so transformative. Once you start looking at people at the end of the thought and hold the gaze for a moment, as if you are checking they get it, your audiences will start to respond in a whole new way because they feel as though you really care about them getting your message.

Eye contact tip: When you are preparing a presentation, underline the key points and draw a little eye symbol at the final words of those key points. That is where you should make eye contact to make the most impact. Remember, it's sustained eye contact, with intention.

LSW Gem: Eye contact

Imagine three speakers, each using different eye contact, each one making a different statement.

Speaker one: They look at the audience in the middle of their sentence and back at their notes for the end of the sentence.

The statement: They are checking that the audience is there or still listening.

Speaker two: They look away before completing the final few words of the sentence.

The statement: Their priority is to keep up speed so that no one is bored.

Speaker three: They make eye contact on the final word or two of the important thought.

The statement: They have one priority: making sure the audience received their ideas.

Eye contact exercise...

There's an exercise that we do with our clients that has powerful effects. Find a friend to do this with or, if you can't, try to film yourself. Read the text below to your friend (or camera) in three ways. Each time you read, do it with as much colour and energy as you can muster.

What General Weyland called the Battle of France is over. I expect that the Battle of Britain is about to begin. Upon this battle depends the survival of Christian civilisation. Upon it depends our own British life and the long continuity of our institutions and our Empire.

Their Finest Hour, Winston Churchill

1. With no eye contact at all.
2. With flicking eye contact in the middle of a sentence, looking down before the final word.
3. With sustained eye contact at the final few words of the sentence before the punctuation, crucially holding eye contact for a beat after the last word has been spoken.

When you have done that, ask the classic communication questions:

Did the speaker care about what they were saying?

Did they care about their listener?

As a result, did the listener care?

EYE CONTACT RESPONSES

This exercise illustrates that eye contact can lead to profound differences not only in the audience's engagement, but also in the judgements the listeners make about the speaker. I have done this hundreds of times and each time I receive the same responses.

With no eye contact: It was tedious. The speaker didn't care about what they were saying. They lacked passion. Neither did they care about their listener and, as a result, the listener does not care.

With flicking eye contact: It was as if the speaker was looking out of duty, or to check the listener was there. The speaker barely cared about the text and certainly didn't have a connection with what they were saying. The speaker had an awkward and ultimately insecure relationship with the listener.

With sustained eye contact at key points: It was interesting and engaging to listen to. The speaker's relationship with the text was passionate and confident, they had ownership over the words. Furthermore, they cared about the listener: they wanted the listener to really understand.

LSW Gem: Who to look at when giving a presentation

You don't need to stare, you don't need to look at everyone. If you have a large audience, sharing your eye contact in different parts of the audienceis a good idea.

Some people swear by the M shape — left front, left back, middle front, right back, right front. Personally, this is too scientific for me. But left, right, middle is a good rule of thumb.

LSW Gem: Eye contact and why we shouldn't stare

When we are speaking, we have power over the attention of our listeners, particularly if we are speaking to just one or two people. If we are staring, they may well stare back and we can become locked into an uncomfortable and counterproductive situation, like two cars heading for each other on a motorway. There won't be any actual collision but it feels like there might be. In this situation, the audience becomes more aware of eye contact than of what the person is saying!

How to break the stare

If you are the speaker, look away from the audience and into the distance as if you are trying to find the appropriate word. Then return to look at your listener at the end of each thought.

If you are the listener, look down and nod to show you are listening, then look back at the speaker at the end of their thought.

Using Your Voice

What goes up, must come down, right? Well the same goes for your voice, particularly when you are trying to deliver your ideas.

Have you ever listened to someone who raises the pitch of their voice at the end of every clause in their sentence? Your brain feels like it's going to explode trying to hold all the units of speech in your mind until you finally lose the thread altogether. What they are doing is called upward inflection. It is very typical of English teenagers and also of Australian speakers, and is difficult for the English ear to listen to. Upward inflection should be used sparingly because it can, in some situations, reduce the value of what you are saying, make the speaker appear less authoritative and even less intelligent. There are only two occasions to use upward inflection: for a list, and for a question that you genuinely don't know the answer to.

Your voice can go up in the middle of a thought, but it needs to come down at the end. A good way to think about it is building a bridge between you and your listener. It starts at you, goes up a little in the middle, then comes down to your listener. We call this vocal gravity. Otherwise it's like trying to deliver while reaching up. Usually, the very act of using a physical example with the delivery (with spoons, for example) ensures people's voices will follow suit. But if you find your voice goes up at the end of your thoughts, this is something you will probably want to work on.

LISTS

The list inflection informs the listener that everything is of equal value; each item has no particular importance in and of itself, but is simply a fraction of the whole. By using the same rhythm and tone to go up with each item, the implicit statement is that they are small, forgettable items that hold no particular importance.

You can see why it might not be beneficial to use upward inflection on ordinary speech!

Shopping list example: I'm going shopping (downward inflection). I'm going to buy potatoes (up), tomatoes (up), bath salts (up), chocolate (up), and a bottle of champagne (down).

If the thoughts that make up a sentence are not important, like in a shopping list, then it's fine to recite them with a list-like tone. However, if those thoughts are important, then we need to reflect their unique value with our voice.

Inflection exercise...

A good example of this reduced value is to take a really interesting list and say it with upward inflection. Each item becomes boring. Try it for yourself with the following two lists.

I went to the supermarket and I bought... a banana, an apple, a dozen eggs, a turkey and a bottle of champagne.

I went to the supermarket and... I found a green monkey in the bakery section, I slid down aisle 12 on my tummy, I waltzed with a cowboy, I squashed a tomato in someone's face and I bought two bags of shopping.

QUESTIONS

The other time we use upward inflection is if we are asking a question to which we really want the answer. It's fine to go up in pitch here because, in a sense, that is admitting that what you're saying isn't complete – it needs an answer to complete it. In this case it can be like reaching out to someone, needing reassurance, a half-thought needing its response to become whole. There is definitely a place for this. Sometimes you might use this inflection to show willing, to connect or reach out to someone. But it will not be useful to create authority or to assert status. If we want to seem certain and sure of ourselves, then we need to deliver our thoughts using vocal gravity or downward inflection.

Build a bridge tip: If you are struggling, it can help to add a flourish of the hand. Literally put your hand in an arc shape as you speak the unit or thought, outlining a bridge between you and the other person.

Be the creator tip: Use facts, or imagine you are God building the earth. Say statements like 'two plus two equals four' with complete certainty, or 'and then there was light'. God wouldn't upward inflect!

Delivering your message to its intended destination
/ GOLDEN RULES /

1. Be clear on the overriding intention of all verbal communication – to reach your listener.

2. When choosing where to make eye contact, it is always on the final words of an important thought.

3. The best eye contact when 'delivering' to an audience is sustained for a beat at the end of a unit, which shows them you genuinely want to ensure they receive the thought.

4. If you are preparing a presentation, underline where you wish to make eye contact, around which ideas it is most important you deliver.

5. Make sure that your voice comes down at the end of a thought, so that the idea really is delivered.

Chapter 5 |Overcoming nerves|

In this chapter you will learn about:

- **Understanding fear:** So we can control it
- **Dealing with common fears:** And what to do about them
- **Practice techniques:** To do in advance of the presentation
- **Before you start:** Techniques to do immediately before the presentation
- **While you are speaking:** Techniques to do during the presentation

When the fear steps in, it dominates our minds so we can hear the voice of fear more loudly than anything else. Once there, it threatens to break the connection with our audience. This is not about our audience – instead we are thinking about ourselves and what could go wrong. For communication to be effective, an energy must be created and maintained between speaker and audience. Fear, being an inward-looking energy, gets in the way of this. By the end of the chapter you will have a better understanding of which fear tugs at your heels, and have a few tricks up your sleeve to fight it off so you can get on with being brilliant.

Case study: Panic attacks

I used to get panic attacks before speaking in public. I loved communicating, but the thought of speaking in a group would take my breath away.

One day I decided to do something about it and went to Toastmasters. After a couple of weeks, I signed myself up to make a speech and began the preparation. When the time came for me to stand up and make the speech, my heart was in my mouth. I felt everyone expected me to be brilliant, so I decided on a different strategy.

> Rather than thinking about impressing anyone, I concentrated on the importance of my message. I let go of any idea of being good. I remember thinking, 'It's from my heart and it's just about connecting with people. It's not being anything other than who I am.'
>
> And then I got up there and it was incredible. I'd let go of all the trying hard and arrived at a simple authenticity, and I was off and away, delighted to share my story. I won the prize that evening, and also won back my confidence in speaking in public.

Understanding Fear

If the need to speak is bigger than the fear, then we'll find a way. If we push against the boundaries of our fears, we can move beyond them. If we believe in our fear too much, keeping within its safe parameters, then it becomes even more fixed. The trick is realising that it's just a story, one that probably came in childhood, and it has either outlived its purpose or was wrong to start with. Knowing that our fears may not represent reality but are just a bit of leftover baggage we never got round to dumping, can be a good first step in dismantling the fear. It doesn't stop it being there, but it does help you not to take it too seriously.

It's also good to know some of the greatest speakers in the world were terrified of public speaking, including Abraham Lincoln and Gandhi. In his autobiography, Gandhi tells of a time when he stood up to speak and was shaking so much he forgot his words. However, both overcame it because their need to speak was greater than their fears.

Finally, there is a strong evolutionary argument for fear of public speaking, and that is because it puts the human in a potential danger zone, singled out and surrounded. This is not, biologically speaking, the safest position to be in. Obviously, it's not actually a life-threatening situation, so the fear is no longer a rational survival mechanism, but the process of dismantling that evolutionary instinct can take a little longer. The good news is it's simply about practice: the more we do, the easier it gets. However, if you're anything like me, you'll want some techniques and strategies to help!

Dealing With Common Fears

Below are some examples of general fears that many people have about public speaking. Notice how they strongly represent the chimp voice, rather than the adult (see Chapter 12). In each case, I've suggested techniques from the following section to use to overcome your nerves. But first, here are three general concepts to understand.

Change your focus: Be outward focused, not self-focused. If you feel fear, try looking outside of you, paying more attention to your listeners and how your message can best serve them, rather than what they think of you.

Change your body: Fear activates a physical fight or flight response. Shoulders curve inwards and arms cross or are pinned to the sides of a rigid body. The hunched spine compresses the diaphragm and leads to shallow breathing and a strained voice. The body's response confirms to the brain that you are fearful and sets up a negative feedback loop. By changing the position of the body, you can send different signals to the brain. For example, rolling your shoulders back and down, stretching out your arms and breathing more deeply changes how you feel. Once that happens, you can start introducing more positive thoughts.

Grasp the opportunity: Focus only on communicating your message. Use all the intonation and delivery techniques you will learn throughout this book and they will hold you firm in the face of your nerves.

FEAR OF MAKING A FOOL OF YOURSELF

When this happens, you are hearing a negative internal voice that tells you you're no good or you'll look like an idiot. A little like a heckler who shouts you down or says mean things when you are going to go for something or take a risk. This is the chimp in quite aggressive form.

Banish the chimp by concentrating on what you want to say, on what the adult would say, or by simply giving it something else to do, like distracting a child. 'Go and stamp on bananas in the corner. I've got a presentation to get on with.'

Techniques to use: Banish the bully, Visualisation, Connection, Golden ball, Power gesture.

FEAR OF FAILURE

This is when you start focusing on what could go wrong and coming up with reasons for not going ahead as there is no point; justifying why failure is likely. Believing in failure is the worst thing.

Anyone who has succeeded in life will tell you that learning from failure is one of the well-known keys to success. Ask your chimp what failure actually looks like – what's the worst that could happen? Could be that it's not so bad after all. Then bring in your rational adult. He might say failure is known to be a great learning opportunity; the likelihood of failure is actually fairly low; or he may come up with ideas to mitigate the possibility of failure.

Techniques to use: Visualisation, Banish the bully, Power gesture.

FEAR OF UNLUCKY GENES OR NOT BEING GOOD ENOUGH

If you believe that you are simply not a good communicator, the likelihood is that you just won't try; you'll playing safe. After all, why bother to put in the energy?

Okay, you may not be someone who instinctively knows how to give a brilliant speech – very few people do. But you can learn the techniques. Practise and you will very quickly see improvement that will boost your confidence.

Techniques to use: Connection, Banish the bully, Change your state, Power gesture and Practice.

Practice Techniques

Here is a series of techniques to try months, weeks or hours before a speech or presentation, or even while you are speaking. Try them out and see which ones work for you.

CONNECTION PHASE 1

Where: A public space will do

How long: At least 15 minutes

This is about using your connection to people and your drive to speak to overcome your nerves. If you really want to communicate your message, you don't need to worry about being a fantastic speaker or impressing people. It doesn't matter if you slip up on a word. The most important thing is that you are authentic and connect with your audience. If you are feeling the pressure, just coming back to this simple, honest reason to speak is very powerful: the more you can build your motivation to speak, the more it will override any fear.

Look at your speech and ask yourself:

*   What are your goals for the audience, or what are you giving to them? Which bits of your speech really share that? Imagine saying those bits simply and beautifully, really sharing them.
*   Which bits of your speech do you feel most passionate about?
*   If they get your message, what will the impact be on your audience? Will they be moved? See something in a new light? Want to sign up to something that will make a difference to their lives? Have relief from pain or fear?

- Come back to the places in your speech that really deliver on these goals and tune into them. Imagine they are gems you will be placing into the hands of the audience.

PRACTICE

Where: Somewhere private

How long: As long as it takes

This seems obvious but is often missed. If you have an important presentation or speech that you want to ace, there is nothing like practice to get you ready for it. Practise it in front of a mirror, practise it for friends. The effect of this practice is that you get used to it, you build muscle memory around it, and you can see quickly where your glitches are. Practise, practise, practise. If you want to practise for presentations or speeches in general, join a speaking club like Toastmasters. Practise with techniques and you will quickly improve.

VISUALISATION

Where: A public space will do

How long: 10 minutes

Some people are sceptical about visualisations but they are, in fact, backed up by scientific research. Psychologists have found that by imagining a physical process, you canbuild neural pathways in your brain that are almost exactly the same as if you had physically done the activity!

There is a lovely example of a concert pianist who was jailed for around a decade, and when he came out, he was even better at playing the piano than before. People asked him how he did it, and he told them it was by practising every day – in his imagination.

Try visualising yourself calmly getting out of your seat and walking up on to the stage, looking at the audience and delivering your speech. Take it all the way to the applause and your sense of triumph. At points, you may start to feel anxious – this is fine, and shows you are in the imagination zone. But you have control! Simply rewind a little and do it again until you don't feel the nerves. This is an incredibly powerful technique and is well worth the concentration it requires.

BANISH THE BULLY

Where: Somewhere private

How long: At least 1 hour

This involves understanding that your fear is a bully. This is a coaching concept that we have saboteurs – or gremlins or bullies (name them as you will) – inside our minds that try to stop us living the life we want. A successful coaching technique is to get to know your internal bully, what it is afraid of, what it says and how it gets at you. You can even give it a name and an image. Then, if and when you hear negative voices, you'll instantly recognise your bully, calmly tell it that you are busy and order it to sit in a corner while you get on with the business of making your life great.

Before You Start

Right, your presentation is 20 minutes away and you have a knot of steel in your stomach. You want to pull a last minute sickie. Here are some great techniques to help you deal with nerves in the last few minutes before the speech.

GOLDEN BALL

Where: Somewhere private

How long: 5 to 10 minutes

Imagine a ball of gold melting in your belly. Let its warmth spread down your legs and radiate up through your chest. With each breath you take into your belly, the ball melts more. With each out breath, the gold spreads further around your body. Roll your shoulders slowly; let the gold ease into your neck. Open your chest and roll your shoulders back. Stretch your arms out. You can do this sitting in a chair just before you need to get up to do the presentation.

POWER GESTURE

Where: Somewhere semi-private

How long: 3 minutes

It has been proven that if you stand in a power position for two minutes, you will significantly reduce your cortisol (stress hormone) and raise your testosterone. So before a presentation, go somewhere private and stand with your arms outstretched and legs open and firmly planted on the ground. Two minutes later, you will feel different. (To understand more about this, visit Chapter 7 and read about Amy Cuddy's Ted Talk.)

CHANGE YOUR STATE

Where: Somewhere semi-private

How long: 3 minutes

This is an extension of the previous technique. You've got to go on stage, you're scared. Change the voices in your head. Yell, dance, get pumped up – think of a boxer before a big fight. That's you! He's got one thought – winning. Find the thing that helps you get into a powerful frame of mind – a gesture or a piece of music maybe – and use that to make you feel like the champion. Have your earphones ready. If you like this technique, watch some YouTube videos featuring Anthony Robbins, America's foremost motivational coach. This is his signature technique.

MEET YOUR CHIMP

Where: Somewhere semi-private

How long: 3 minutes

This is based on the book, *The Chimp Paradox* by Steve Peters. It states that we are made up of two parts, the chimp and the adult. The chimp comes from the original brain and chiefly has appetites and the fight or flight response. The adult, on the other hand, comes from the neocortex, is rational and reasonable. There is a place for both of them in our personality, but most of the time, the adult is way better. In high-pressure situations the chimp can be particularly annoying and get in the way, taunting us with our worst fears.

The thing to do, says the author, is to simply recognise who is doing the talking and then acknowledge if it's the chimp. There are two simple and effective steps:

1. Ask yourself who is doing the talking – the chimp or the adult?

2. If you locate the chimp, ask yourself what the adult would say.

This allows you to separate the rational from the irrational rather than feeling like you are the thoughts in your head.

LABELLING YOUR PHYSICAL STATE

Where: A public space will do

How long: 3 minutes

So you are feeling nervous, your heart is pumping, your breathing is fast and, quite frankly, you'd rather be almost anywhere else but here. Fine. With this technique, you take notice of and label each of your physical symptoms in your mind, somehow, by acknowledging them, half their sting seems to leave.

While You Are Speaking

Sometimes the nerves kick in in the middle of presentations or speeches, but it doesn't have to ruin them. There are steps you can take to regain control and make sure you keep your presentations powerful.

CONNECTION PHASE 2

This is linked to Connection phase 1 (see above). Take the first moment on stage to connect to your audience. See them as individuals. In that moment of connection, let the relationship dynamic change from you and them to a shared space, where they are giving to you and you are giving to them.

FOCUS ON YOUR AUDIENCE

Remember that your energy follows where you put your focus, so focus on your listeners and on delivering your ideas to them well and you will forget your nerves and be back on track. If a thought about impressing other people or not being good enough creeps in, bat it away like a fly.

IMAGINE YOUR AUDIENCE IS FASCINATED

Simply imagine the audience is fascinated by what you are saying. If you hear any counter-thought, kick it out and replace it with their thrilled faces. They are hanging on your every word. Start having fun with your speech, enjoying yourself, taking the time you need. And chances are the audience will become more and more interested.

USE A MEMORY GUIDE

It might also help to prepare a memory guide: bullet points to guide you through your sequence. Associate the bullet points with a physical object and then link the objects together in the order of the bullets to tell a story. Somehow this sticks in your memory more than the order of bullets. There are some books specifically on these techniques. Personally, while I have learnt them, I have never needed to use them, but many people swear by them!

HAVE AN OBJECTIVE

It could be to speak with passion, to emphasise key words in delivery, to evoke certain feelings in the audience; whatever it is, get really clear on your objective, and then pursue it like a heat-seeking missile. When our heads are filled with our mission, there is no room for fear.

Psychology says that we can't think two opposing thoughts at one time. Try grinning broadly, right now, ear to ear. Count to five, still grinning. Holding that grin, think of something sad. It's not easy. That's because your brain is receiving signals that it is happy. So in a presentation, if panic sets in, simply focus on emphasis, or delivering your ideas (or any of the basic tools) and let that shift your mind from fear-based thoughts.

FIND THE RIGHT WORD

If you find yourself in the middle of a thought, and you realise you don't know what to say next, remember that no one expects you to speak in elegant prose every time you open your mouth; this is not a script. You could berate yourself for not having the right word to hand, or you could praise yourself for being a perfectionist – not a difficult choice! Breathe. Take the time you need, calmly and confidently. Find the perfect word or phrase to convey your meaning. Remember the power of pauses.

Overcoming nerves
/ GOLDEN RULES /

1. Fear is a natural instinct but it is no longer useful in this context.

2. An antidote to nerves is good communication, so get your objective clear and focus on your audience.

3. Practise, be it through visualisations or the real thing, to get your brain accustomed to the speech and give you confidence.

4. Remember to choose the preparation techniques you find effective and use them just before and during the presentation.

5. It is useful to understand our fears but we should know they are often unfounded. Once you understand them, use your adult brain to combat the fears.

PART 2

Understanding
non-verbal communication

Chapter 6 | The magic of connection spaces |

In this chapter you will learn about:

- **Intimate connection space:** The gentle, sensitive space

- **Relaxed connection space:** Familiar and confident space

- **Performance connection space:** Putting on a show

- **Transformational connection space:** Spreading your energy

- **Connection spaces and presentations:** How to use the method to enhance performance

- **One-to-one connection spaces:** How to use the method in small groups

The Serlin Method™ of connection spaces offers a really useful shorthand to finding your own physical and vocal range. They frame and articulate four different ways of connecting with other people to help you step out of your typical way of communicating, your comfort zone, into a zone appropriate to your message and your audience. Each of the zones has its individual kind of gesture and energy.

A GOOD WAY TO THINK ABOUT connection spaces is like a different outfit you might put on – the sharp suit for an important meeting, the soft cashmere or silk of a date by candle light, the tracksuit and cotton t-shirt for a lazy Sunday afternoon – all of these will create a mini physical environment for us to adjust to.

Similarly, we all have different aspects of our characters. An animal lover will show their soft side when they see a cute puppy, but as a manager of a football team they'll show a robust and dominant side. The connection space tool acts as a shortcut to access those different outfits, and different aspect of ourselves, in seconds – without having to go into the wardrobe!

Intimate Connection Space

You might want to create this space if you want to draw in your listeners, have them listen more intently and with increased focus. It is also a more gentle, sensitive space; you could be sharing something personal here, or something that has more gravitas and significance. The kind of attention you are demanding from your listeners is higher quality. When you create this kind of space, you should be able to hear a pin drop. Everyone feels responsible for holding the silence.

You need to earn this kind of space, which has an intimacy that the others don't have. Sometimes, you will notice this space in the theatre, when the audience is totally quiet and they are sharing a moment with the characters, almost holding their breath. This is the most precious kind of space, because everyone is working together to hold it, no matter how many people there are.

You can show this intimate space in your body with stillness, a more intense gaze, leaning in, and really intently delivering your ideas.

The pictures below show two speakers in an intimate connection space. You can imagine if you were to hear either of these people in these moments, their voices would be low, their pace relatively slow and their tone of voice would be quite gentle. Notice how while the two pictures are very different there is a sense of something private being shared.

Figure 6.1

Intimate space

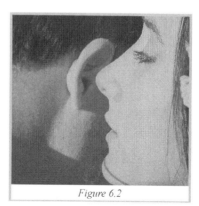

Figure 6.2

Intimate space

INTIMATE CONNECTION SPACE

Posture: Leaning in.

Eyes: Sincere, focused, direct.

Gesture: Small, simple, arms and hands close to body.

Vocal tone: Slow, low voice, limited tonal range.

Content: Serious, secretive, delicate, private.

Situation: High stakes, serious, really connecting to people, sensitive.

Relaxed Connection Space

This space is relaxed and more familiar. A very good, easy, confident and relaxed public speaker will hang out in this place a lot. It's as if they are chatting to a friend and yet they can hold the attention of hundreds. The speaker uses light, easy gestures, with moderate use of hands and arms; the hands can be in the pocket or lightly gesticulating. The body is relaxed and open. It's important to have confident body language and posture here, as you won't be able to hold the attention of a large crowd without it.

The kind of attention you have from the audience here will be relaxed and open, engaged and maybe nodding along a little. The audience will be sitting in their seats, maybe leaning back or in an informal pose, possibly leaning on their knees. They will feel engaged but not on high alert.

This kind of connection is useful for building an easy rapport with the audience, and is great for telling anecdotes or jokes. It's where you can show them who you are in a relaxed way, reveal your personality and get them on side. It is a friendly, bonding place, and is suited to smiles and warmth, relaxed eye gestures.

In the pictures below you see two speakers in the relaxed connection space.

Figure 6.3

Relaxed space

Figure 6.4

Relaxed space

Both have loose shoulders, relaxed chests and are only using one hand. All of this relaxes their look and message. They are smiling and their eyes are connecting with their audience, but in a softer way than the intimate space.

RELAXED CONNECTION SPACE

Posture: Upright, relaxed.

Eyes: Relaxed, moving around, in imagination and with audience.

Gesture: Relaxed gestures, hands in pockets, swinging by side, natural.

Vocal tone: Colourful, light, medium volume, warm.

Content: Jokey, relaxed, friendly, anecdotal, informative.

Situation: Social situations, small presentations to colleagues, moments in a presentation to a larger audience and interviews.

Performance Connection Space

This is where the social performance comes in. Speakers here will take bigger strides across the stage, their elbows will be at least an outstretched hand's width from their sides, and hands will be moving in strong, expressive gestures. If they are speaking to a smaller group where confidence levels are high, their voice is bold and the intention is to make impact. There is nothing timid or shrinking violet about this space. Gestures and facial expressions are big, and the intention is to hold the attention of a crowd. This space is big enough for several, even if the person is only speaking to one. The tone of voice has colour and range, and volume is louder than normal. In terms of gears, it's third or fourth gear.

Notice in the pictures below how both the speakers have big demonstrative gestures and their elbows are some distance from their bodies. There is no slouching here, and there is a sense of controlled performance from both of them. Their gaze and facial expressions are strong and their energy and delivery spreads outward.

Figure 6.5

Performance space

Figure 6.6

Performance space

PERFORMANCE CONNECTION SPACE

Posture: Upright, shoulders back. No slouching here!

Eyes: Direct, wide, strong.

Gesture: Arms away from sides, strong gesture, focused fingers.

Vocal tone: Strong volume, full use of vocal range, well-projected voice, emphasis. Speed varied but between slow and fast.

Content: Higher stakes, important information.

Situation: Large presentations, pitches and product launches.

Transformational Connection Space

In the transformational space, it's really big. It's owning all the space around you and then some. It's spreading your energy out far and wide and with intention and direction.

There is nothing intimate about this space, but it is powerful. How do you get here? Well, you need to rev yourself up to this space as your message is going to be pretty big. Arm gestures will be extravagant, face will be free, and chances are if you do get to this space, you're going to be pretty passionate so your body will be taking over anyway!

The attention of the audience here should be totally with you, it's a rallying space to be in, the kind where you are buoyed on the energy of the crowd. It's a joint effort to get you to this space, and by the time you have arrived, there is so much energy around you that you don't know what's yours and what's theirs. This is the space where charismatic politicians and motivational speakers work from. Political figures and motivational speakers spend a fair bit of time in this space, rousing their audiences into action.

Figure 6.7

Transformational space

Figure 6.8

Transformational space

Look at the pictures above – you can see the intensity of facial expression and the engagement of their entire bodies. You can feel everyone will be with the speaker. Their faces show emotion, even anguish. As you can see, the transformational space is where passion takes over! The power of this kind of connection is that the audience and speaker become interdependent and connected.

TRANSFORMATIONAL CONNECTION SPACE

Posture: Upright.

Eyes: Alive.

Gesture: Huge.

Vocal tone: Loud, extensive tonal range.

Content: Highest stakes, bigger themes, sense of purpose.

Situation: Public speeches, political rallies.

Connection Spaces And Presentations

The connection spaces are a brilliant way to shape your presentation. As we know, movement helps to shape a speech for people, and to stick it in their memories. So moving through phases of intimacy, relaxed and performance can be useful in terms of keeping the presentation varied. The best way of using connection spaces is to define the mood you want to convey in the different parts of your speech, or the energy of each section, and let your body articulate that via the connection spaces.

It might be that you have a space where you are most comfortable. For me, it's the relaxed space. For another person it might be the intimate space. That is fine, assume you will spend most of the presentation in that comfortable space, then have a look at where there might be a need for a change. Look at the writing style that suits each space.

Intimate connection space: When the message is quite serious, and you want to be really still and have no other distraction. The stakes are quite high around this message and it's packed with meaning.

Relaxed connection space: Perfect for anecdotes, general chats and getting people into the swing of things. Can be a powerful contrast with intimate so you can use this to create effect.

Performance connection space: More formal and larger, this is great for a bigger speech to a bigger audience, or simply to really hold people's attention. It's a bit larger than life and works for most texts to a larger audience. It doesn't really work with a small room and less than three people, though!

Transformational connection space: This is really only for huge events with huge stakes requiring huge energy. The message is transformational, it's rock concert or change the world territory!

Case study: Connection spaces

A client called Amy was a finance director in the City, and she was extremely clever and very shy. She spent most of her communication in the intimate connection space. This was how she spoke to her family, her colleagues, her team and in meetings. She came to London Speech Workshop because she had difficulty asserting authority with members of her team. She was terrified of meetings as she disliked having the attention on her, and she used to apologise continuously. Many of her sentences started with an apology.

She wanted to manage her team with more power, to communicate in meetings more effectively, to be more confident: she wanted to sound different but not feel fake.

The huge shift came for her when she began working with connection spaces. When she took on the performance space, the difference was huge. Not only did it change her delivery, her tone of voice, her whole body language, but her content changed too. She no longer began her sentences with an apology, she framed things differently. A little practice and not only did she become adept at slipping into the performance space, she enjoyed it. And the results were dramatic. As she began to speak up in meetings, the other directors started involving her more, asking her to speak and contribute. Her staff also responded positively and her confidence levels soared.

Connection Spaces And One-To-One Communication

Through working with connection spaces at London Speech Workshop, we found it's an amazing tool for working on all communication, not just pre-pared speeches. It gives you an easy way to access more of yourself and to find how different spaces can be of benefit in different situations. Because it's so simple, everyone can explore the different spaces. Interestingly, as with the case study above, when you practise you will find it has an effect on so much more than just your gesture. It changes the words you use, the expressions you make, your volume, pace of speaking and tone.

If you think about the goal of your communication, you can therefore make a more informed decision about choosing the space that will lead to the best possible outcome. For example, let's say you are an actor meeting new agents. You want them to take you seriously, see that you are confident and capable, and ultimately sign you up. Through practising the different spaces, you find that the best one for you is performance with a bit of relaxed thrown in. From that place you feel confident and empowered, while you know that habitually you might have gone in a little more shy and subdued.

Remember, this is never about losing authenticity, it's about finding your range through having a simple tool to apply.

Let's say you have something really important to say to someone. Try practising it using the connection space tool to see what different connection spaces offer you. If you find, for example, you are naturally very authoritative and yet struggle to make more intimate connections, you'll benefit from practising the intimate space. Similarly, if you know your habitual space is intimate and you do well in one-to-one or small groups but find larger groups more challenging, then the performance space will be a useful resource for you.

Connection spaces exercise...

Using the text below, **start in intimate and work through the spaces, going to relaxed, then performance** and finally (and if you want to try it) **transformational.** Switch to a different space every few lines, and see how easy it is, and what fun it is. I have purposely picked a text that is quite dense and also quite humorous, so you can concentrate on style over meaning.

I think it was that very fine and subtle writer, Vernon Lee, who lapsed into literary heresy by saying that a poet is always a pantheist. I could only accept this in the amended form that no poet, by any possibility, has ever been or ever will be a pantheist. It was precisely because Walt Whitman sometimes tried on principle to be a pantheist, that so great a genius just missed being a poet; but Shelley did not miss being a poet; but he did miss being a pantheist.

A deep imaginative instinct, beyond all his cheap philosophies, made him always do something which is the soul of imagination, but the very opposite of universalism. It made him insulate the object of which he wrote; making the cloud or the bird as solitary as possible in the sky. imagination demands an image. An image demands a background. The background should be equal and level, or vast and vague, but only for the sake of the image. In writing of the skylark Shelley compares that unfortunate wild fowl to a lady in a tower, to a star, to a rose, to all sorts of things that are not in the least like a skylark. But they all have one touch, the touch of separation and solitude.

The Spice of Life and Other Essays, GK Chesterton

Role-play exercise...

If you would rather go straight into a role play, this is also quite good practice – and even better if you can find a friend to try it with. Either try a conversation you have coming up – say, giving some difficult feedback to someone at work, or **choose a role play from the examples below.**

- You are a director of a small company of eight staff. It is near Christmas, and you notice that within one day the office cabinet has been conspicuously depleted of tape, scissor and packing materials. Apart from you, the administrative assistant, Julie, is the only one with the key to the cabinet. You will need to have a talk with Julie.

- You are the secretary of a local charity group. You asked the assistant secretary, John, to work immediately on the minutes of an important meeting and then send to your boss for her review. The next day, the society's president gives you a hard time for not getting her the information as requested. This doesn't make you look good. You decide to talk to John.

- You are a head teacher supervising 15 teachers and support staff. For the school to function well, it needs a collaborative environment where the teachers give guidance and direction to the support staff. One of the teachers, Katie, has started dating a person on the support staff. Although there is no policy prohibiting dating, several members of staff have complained about the two being too affectionate in the staff room. Some also indicate there is preferential treatment for Katie's new-found love interest. You need to talk to Katie.

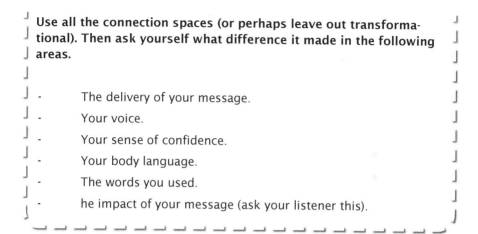

Use all the connection spaces (or perhaps leave out transformational). Then ask yourself what difference it made in the following areas.

- The delivery of your message.
- Your voice.
- Your sense of confidence.
- Your body language.
- The words you used.
- he impact of your message (ask your listener this).

These two exercises are useful to start you thinking about your habitual space and what you can gain from exploring other spaces. For so many of our clients, it is a real eye-opener, as they learn their go-to places, and get ideas on what else there is available to them.

The magic of connection spaces
/ GOLDEN RULES /

1. There are four different kind of connection space, each of which suits a different type of situation or relationship.

2. You will have a habitual space where you feel most comfortable.

3. When you are in a different space, it changes not just your non-verbal communication, but also the words you use and how you speak.

4. When you are giving a presentation or speech, use a range of connection spaces to keep your speech interesting and your audience engaged.

5. Use connection spaces to broaden your range and find new ways of dealing with difficult situations.

Chapter 7 | How to use your body for effect |

In this chapter you will learn about:

- **Body awareness:** Knowing what your body language is saying
- **Power positions:** Using your body to exert control
- **Posture:** And the importance of standing well
- **How to use gesture:** Body talk
- **Fitting the words to the gestures:** Making sure you give a single message
- **Using no gestures at all**

I don't like to hear a cut and dried sermon. When I hear a man preach, I like to see him act as if he were fighting bees.

Abraham Lincoln

Another crucial technique in your armoury is how to use your body and, in particular, your hands, to improve your communication. Good posture is a crucial component of non-verbal communication and we'll help you find that. Then we'll discover how to engage with gesture and hear the difference gesture makes to your voice.

MUCH OF THIS BOOK IS ABOUT BEING IN CHARGE of the impression you give to others. It's giving you concrete tools so that you can come across in a way that makes you feel and appear confident and grounded. What happens then is an upward spiral – people treat you as if you are confident and grounded, and then you feel more confident and grounded.
A popular statistic is that about 93% of the impression we make comes through our non-verbal communication, and about 55% of that is through our body. While this may not be entirely accurate, and the value of content is always relevant, it is important to take into account how much of our message is portrayed not through our words but through our body and voice. So we want to make sure that our body is saying what we want it to say.

DID YOU KNOW?

Words are not enough

The figure 55% comes from Albert Mehrabian, who undertook research on communication in 1971, the results of which are still often quoted today. Mehrabian came to the conclusion that face-to-face communication consisted of words, tone and body language. Words (the literal meaning) account for 7% of the overall message, tone of voice accounts for 38% of the overall message and body language accounts for 55% of the overall message. However, he pointed out that these percentages are relevant only when a person is talking about their feelings or attitudes.

What we don't want is for our words to be saying one thing, our voice and manner of speaking to be saying another, and our body to be saying another thing entirely! Fortunately, it is possible to become aware of the messages you are giving out with your body language and then make sure they are consistent with the messages you want to convey.

Case study: A lecture on astrophysics can go either way...

You are at a conference and you don't recognise the name of the next keynote speaker. It's an hour-long session on the magic of astrophysics. This could go either way...

You wait for the speaker to enter the room and you notice how she avoids eye contact with the audience, her shoulders are curved and her hands are fidgeting. You can almost feel her nerves as she stands in front of the podium. Within her first 30 seconds of entry, the speaker has dug a hole for herself that is going to be a struggle to emerge

from. You and your fellow audience members have probably all experienced a similar slump as you picture the hour of tedium ahead.

The unconscious messages she shared were fear, awkwardness and not wanting to be there. Her body expressed that foremost on her mind was not the importance of her messages but her fears of how she would be perceived. She has given you permission to opt out.

She could be a genius with so much to say – but she's going to have a bit of a mountain to climb to show you as much.

Now let's look at the opposite scenario. The same person has read this book and this time she walks in with her shoulders back, her spine erect. She makes eye contact with the audience and nods or smiles a little. She goes to the lectern, takes a moment to acknowledge her audience by looking around the room, and then begins to speak.

How receptive are you now?

Body Awareness

Understanding body language means that you can be more in control of the impression you give out. If, for example, you are feeling particularly nervous and defensive and about to go into a tough meeting, you can make sure your body language is expressing confidence and openness so you give a positive impression to the people around you.

Have a look at the box below. Think about where your habitual position is for each component. If you think any of your non-verbal communication is in the defensive column, see if you can start making a conscious choice to change it. If you are not sure, try and take a moment when communicating to do a quick mental check list – where are your shoulders? What are your eyes doing? Perhaps you're usually in the confident column, but some people or situations make you defensive. Try noticing when you are moving into the defensive zone, and what you habitually do when you are feeling defensive, then see if you can change it.

Body	Defensive	Relaxed	Confident and strong
Posture	Shoulders rounded, bent over, small	Shoulders relaxed, not forward or back	Stand up straight with shoulders back
Eye contact	Avoiding eye contact, blinking frequently	Light eye contact, sometimes flitting, sometimes present, easy	Make solid and direct eye contact

Facial expression	Stiff, inexpressive face. Jaw clenching, lip biting	Smiling, bright eyes	Your face is relaxed and warm
Gestures	Small and close to the body or no gestures at all. Arms crossed in front of body	Flowing, easy gestures, relaxed and loose	Firm hand and arm gestures with purpose and intent

DID YOU KNOW?

Body language – crossing your arms

Arm crossing tends to mean you are feeling defensive or self-protective. It is a real giveaway, and should be avoided unless you specifically want to signal that you are closed and/or wary.

Tilting your head to one side can signal trust or feeling safe with someone because by doing so you expose part of your neck, making you vulnerable. As such, it is unusual to tilt your head with people you don't feel comfortable with.

One arm crossed in front of your body can give the impression you are shy and self protecting.

Look at the pictures below. When you know what you are looking for, it is so easy to start to read body language.

Figure 7.1
Defensive body language

Figure 7.2
Confident body language

The first picture has the classic self-protecting position, with shoulders slumped forward slightly. The second shows shoulders back, a relaxed and confident position.

Power Positions

Everywhere in the animal kingdom, postures that enhance an animal's stance makes them appear more powerful.

- When cats are threatened, they freeze, arch their back and fluff out their fur and their tails (making them appear larger).

- Chimpanzees hold their breath and bulge out their chests to seem more powerful.

- Male peacocks fan their tails to attract a mate.

Of course, we are part of the same animal kingdom so the same applies. If we strike a powerful posture, we appear more confident and make a stronger impression. Powerful postures tend to be about making yourself larger, taking your shoulders back and fanning your arms out or clasping your hands behind your head with your elbows to the side.

Below is a fascinating study on the effect of power postures by Amy Cuddy, a highly regarded psychologist from Princeton University.

DID YOU KNOW?

The power position and its two-way influence

In her popular Ted Talk, Amy Cuddy explores the science of body language and how our physical stance can affect not just how others see us, but how we feel about ourselves. Her journey started when she was teaching at Harvard. She noticed that there was a gender split in the grades of the students, and that this split was around participation. She saw that the men tended to get higher grades than the women for participation. She noticed their positions in the class differed, and began to suspect that this was indicative of something. The men would sit in powerful positions, chests out, shoulders back, legs and arms open, while the women tended to sit in less powerful positions, arms crossed, legs crossed, hunched over or shoulders inwards.

In the animal kingdom, animals express power and dominance by becoming bigger, opening up their bodies, and expanding. In humans, it is a similar rule: big is better. We show our status through our stance. However, Amy Cuddy began to suspect it wasn't just the impression on others that a powerful posture was making, but the impression on oneself. She was interested in exploring two specific questions:

Can posture affect how we feel about ourselves?

Can we be influenced by our own non-verbal cues?

She set up some experiments to test this hypothesis. In her study, students were asked to sit or stand in powerful or non-powerful positions for two minutes. Those who stood with arms outstretched and legs wide, for example, not only felt more confident but their bodies showed a chemical reaction supporting that confidence. They measured two specific hormones – cortisol and testosterone. They found that after a mere two minutes of holding a power position, the testosterone hormone (typically associated with male dominance and status) went up and the cortisol hormone (typically associated with stress) went down.

Amy's findings were of sufficient interest to shake up not just the scientific community but the world beyond.

Furthermore, they found these power gestures – such as just two minutes standing in a bathroom arms akimbo – influenced others in an interview situation. In mock interviews, evaluators said, without exception, they would hire those who had taken on a powerful position for two minutes prior to the interview.

Source: TED Global 2012 Amy Cuddy: Your Body Language Shapes Who You Are, June 2012

As we see clearly from this study, our body language doesn't just affect the listener, but also the speaker. This is a recurring theme. What we do physically affects how we feel emotionally and mentally. So if you are sitting or standing slumped, you are going to struggle to feel confident and full of energy. Likewise, if you are standing in a powerful position, shoulders back and body ready, you will struggle to feel small and unprepared.

Posture

If we straighten our spine and let our shoulders go back, we give the impression of openness, readiness and confidence. If our shoulders are slumped, even subtlely, it can give a dramatically different impression. The difference can be very subtly.

Look at the two pictures below and answer the following questions

Figure 7.3
Shoulders slumped

Figure 7.4
Shoulders back

- If one of these people was to be your opponent in an intellectual debate that you wanted to win, who would you rather it be?
- If one of these people was announced as your lawyer for an important case that you wanted to win, who would you rather it be?

You probably chose the first picture for your opponent and the second picture for your lawyer. If this was a situation in real life, you might have no idea why. You might think it was something they said, or you might say they just seemed more confident, or they seemed weaker. The fact is, just that little slump in the shoulders can make all the difference to how we come across.

DID YOU KNOW?

Posture affects self-esteem

Studies have shown that good posture leads to increased self-esteem, and in some studies, people experiencing depression felt markedly better after they madeconcerted efforts to improve their posture.
A study by researchers at Ohio State University instructed subjects to sit up straight or to slouch. The subjects who sat up straight had more confidence in their own thoughts, whether they were positive or negative.

Therapist Dr Heidi Heron says: *The physiology of a person lacking confidence is shifted down in terms of their breathing, posture and gaze. It's like standing and trying to go into a foetal position.*[1]

HOW TO HAVE GOOD POSTURE

Step one: Centre of gravity

Become conscious of your habitual posture, noticing what's going on between your feet and your head. Experiment by pushing your hips forwards and then backwards as you walk, before bringing your hips again to the centre. That's where you want them, as though a plumb line is coming from your head through your body and down to the floor. Think about letting your body find its way into a comfortable balance: your feet connected to the earth and the lightness of your head coming up from the shoulders.

Step two: Alignment

Imagine a string is pulling upwards from the crown of your head to the sky and the rest of your body is hanging down from that string, nudging you into alignment. Your chin should feel balanced, as if it is resting nicely on a little table; not tilted upwards (which strains your voice as you have less direct access to your breath) or downwards.

Step three: Shoulders

Lift your shoulders to your ears and, rolling them back, let the shoulder blades slide down your back. Think about elongating the space between your ear lobes and your shoulders.

Now gently stroke outwards with your hands horizontally across your chest to the edges of your shoulders and feel your chest opening to the world. You should experience a release of tension and feel open and ready.

Try walking in this position and see how it feels.

Open your wings: The three-second trick is to stroke your shoulders back with your hands, opening them up as if they were unfurling wings.

How To Use Gesture

When we use our hands and body to tell our story, as well as our words and voice, our messages become clearer, more engaging and more powerful.Our bodies can create the landscape for our communication. By changing position, we can signal a change of subject. We can separate ideas by moving around to different areas of the stage. The involvement of the body brings an authenticity to the speech because the body is literally describing the scene as well. The other effect is increased engagement from the audience, so they will tend to remember the speech or story better because gestures can act as anchor points in the memory.

THE STARTING LINE

The first rule of gesture is to put yourself in a position where your body can get involved. If, for example, you step onto a stage and put your hands in your pockets or cross your arms, it's going to be difficult to make meaningful gestures. So begin in a state of readiness.

Figure 7.5
State of readiness

For example, starting your presentation with your arms hanging down can be challenging as it can seem like a large distance between your hands and your navel. A good tip is to walk onto the stage with your arms bent at your elbows and, if you like, you can rest one hand in another in line with your navel. This is a good position of readiness as your hands can spring out into gesture easily from there. This space, from your navel and above, is actually your performance space. So that is where you want your hands to be for any presentation or speech.

Try it now: Hold one hand in the other, then spring both hands out, as if to say 'it's here'. That's an easy and relaxed position to start with. To practise, you can try in front of a mirror, perhaps reading a poem and using your arms to shape the scene or tell a story.

POSITIVE HAND GESTURES

Firm fingers: It's important to keep your hands quite firm with your fingers held together, so your energy reaches to the tips of your fingers. **Fists** and strong hands: Both fists and solid hands give an impression of strength and determination, so make sure your hands have strength, particularly for meetings or presentations.

Open hands: A strong gesture that also displays integrity.

Bent elbows: Have your arms bent at the elbows so you can move your hands easily and naturally.

HAND GESTURES TO AVOID

Floppy hands: Imagine you are watering some roses in your garden, let your hands be the hose, and powerfully jet out water so you can reach the roses. We don't want 'floppy hands' where you get a dribble of water at your feet!

Clasping your hands: If you clasp your hands around your navel this can lead to them getting stuck. And in a high-pressured and self-conscious situation, it's very odd how hands can suddenly become nuisance appendages that get in the way!

Clamped elbows: Avoid the elbows getting clamped to your sides as this restricts your hands.

Arms straight and hanging down: This makes it difficult to raise your hands to gesture.

THE IMPORTANCE OF USING GESTURES

At LSW, we use an exercise that works consistently well, even with clients who tend to cut off from their bodies in pressurised situations and speak only with their mouths moving, not using their bodies. Try the exercise yourself to discover how effective it is.

Story of a journey exercise...

Either film yourself, or ask someone to film you, telling a story of journey you have made (or use the suggestion below). As with most of our exercises, you are going to try it two ways.

Step one

First, read the story to get the idea (or use your own), as you will tell your friend or the camera in your own words.

Step two

Recount your chosen story in your own words without gesture; literally sit on your hands if it helps to keep them still.

Step three

Tell the same story, but this time let your hands go and use them to describe the events. This is quite a physical story to give you plenty of gesture opportunities, so if you choose your own story, make sure it has similar qualities.

I was on my way home from work the other night, and I was on the bus, when someone very large sat down beside me. They were so large I found myself squished to the side of the seat and right up against the window. I decided it was best to change seats, but they had earphones on and couldn't hear me. Eventually I realised I had to prod them, so I did. But bizarrely, they didn't feel anything. I prodded harder and, again, nothing! Meanwhile, people behind me were laughing and I was panicking I'd miss my stop.

Finally I gave the person a much bigger shove. They turned around, and I thought I was about to get in real trouble. But it was a guy with a very thin face. He took off his earphones and said, 'I'm so sorry, were you trying to get my attention? I'm wearing a fat suit so I can't feel a thing...' I burst out laughing, along with the people behind me, and managed to get out of the seat and down the stairs, feeling foolish and amused at the same time.

Step four

Once you have finished, watch back the two films and ask yourself the three classic questions of each version:

- Did I, the speaker, care about what I was saying?

- Did I care about you, my audience?

- Did my audience care?

Notice what you found. I also want you to notice the following:

- Did you feel different?

- Did you use different words in the two versions?

Which did you prefer telling? You can also listen back to the two films first, without watching them. You will be able to hear quite distinctly the difference in your voice in each of the two versions. Most of the time, using gesture brings our voice to life, slows us down, makes us sound more interesting and engaged. Another fantastic case for getting your body involved.

When I work with clients on this exercise, we find the same thing all the time. When the speaker is doing the non-gesturing version they find that in order to resist moving, theirwhole body seems literally to shut down. The vocal tone becomes less varied, their facial expression is reduced and, in order to avoid using their hands, they retreat inwards and give much less energy to their speech.

Fitting The Words To The Gestures

Gestures are often our bodies' way of expressing our feelings. But we can also work from the outside in. Look at the gestures below and try them for yourself. Notice how your body will attach meaning to the gesture and, as you move, come up with a line that fits the gesture. See if it makes you feel and communicate differently and how close you are to the words I have suggested.

Eleven hand gestures	Meaning	Words to match	Hand gestures
The fist	Great for big speeches and big ideas when a lot of emphasis is needed.	'We are not going to stand for this treatment any more.'	
The pointing finger	Can be used for specific points but should be used with caution as it's a slightly awkward position that can be difficult to make authentic and can also be considered rude in some Asian cultures.	'The one thing we have to consider is …'	
The splayed fingers and strong hands	This is a very powerful and useful gesture that implies a real connection to your words and has a lot of energy.	'This idea we are grappling with…'	

Hands close together in clapping position	Can be used for explaining specific or more complex ideas.	'It's a very precise process.'	
Fingers close together	This is quite an exact move, as if it's small but important. It could be drawing people's attention to one single idea.	'It's an important detail.'	
Palms facing away from you	A semi-defensive position, as if to say, 'I've done what I can, it's over to you now.' Please use this with caution as it is also considered rude in some cultures.	'You have to work with me.'	
Hands in different positions	Can create contrast, useful for describing two concepts or a relationship between two things.	'It's somehow in conflict.'	

Hands in a steeple position	Can show a sense of ease and pensiveness. A good thinking position, but watch you don't get stuck here.	'I'm delighted to report that…'	
The slice	This gesture is very strong and directive, as if one is cutting through the fluff to get to the sharp truth.	'You better believe…'	
Hands towards the chest	Bringing yourself and your own sincerity about the subject into the audience's awareness.	'I will take personal responsibility.'	

Using No Gestures At All

Interestingly, fear has a very similar effect on the body as asking someone to use no gestures. It clamps down on your system, makes you smaller, and reduces your vocal and expressive range, which means that if you use your gestures when you are nervous, they can help you to bypass the fear effect. By pushing yourself to free up your arms and hands in a speech, you will find that your body and voice also free up. And it is likely to reduce your fear, too, as it will send confident signals to your brain.

You might find gesture comes naturally to you, or you might find that it feels a few steps out of your comfort zone and a little awkward. This is when the notion of social performance comes into play. If you habitually operate in gear two, gesture is probably around gear three and four for you. It's a brilliant tool to be able to have access to, when occasion demands it. At the same time, if your regular gears work well for you in most situations, then there is no need to use it. The idea of this chapter and, in fact, the entire book, is to give you more tools for your tool box, so that you can do more, stretch further, achieve greater things with your communication. Remember, it's not about changing your personality. It's about making a few significant changes to expand your communication horizons. Listen to yourself, and start practising. Your brain will soon be sending you signals as to whether it is working or not – as you'll find you feel brighter, more relaxed and engaged!

How to use your body for effect
/ GOLDEN RULES /

1. Be aware of your body position – where your arms are, how far back your shoulders are – because people will read it!

2. If you are going for an interview or an important presentation, try to spend two minutes beforehand in a power posture – it is scientifically proven to make a difference!

3. The smallest movement forward or back in your shoulders can make all the difference, so if you are doing something important, stroke your shoulders back!

4. Gesture helps your audience to anchor ideas in their memory as it tells a physical story.

5. Incorporating gesture will change your vocal quality and make you appear more connected to what you are saying.

Chapter 8 | Facial expression to influence and captivate |

In this chapter you will learn about:

- **Communicating with your eyes:** The windows to the soul
- **Just smile:** And the world smiles with you
- **Other facial expressions:** And how to use them correctly

So much of how we think and feel is expressed in our face. There are more muscle and nerve endings here than almost any part of our body so it makes sense to put some attention here. A bright smile reflected in your eyes can have a huge impact on a listener so it pays to learn how to apply its contagious power.

MANY PEOPLE AUTOMATICALLY USE A LOT of facial expression and if this is you, then you may think this section is common sense. However, some people reading this will express very little with their face, and if that is the case for you, then this section will be very useful indeed. This may be cultural, or a long-established childhood survival instinct. Perhaps as a child, you learned to hide away what you really thought and felt so that your face didn't give you away. In some situations, playing poker, for example, this can be very useful. And yet, being able to use your facial expression as a communication tool is invaluable.

When you activate your eyes and face while communicating, you are sending signals to your brain that you are in an animated state and that you feel safe enough to reveal yourself through your expressions. As a result, you feel more relaxed and engaged, and you are likely to use more interesting words and images to express yourself. The good news is you can learn how to do this.

Communicating With Your Eyes

Communication is a living, breathing, interactive phenomenon. It's not staid or predictable; it feeds and grows from what is given and what is received. It is said that the eyes are the windows to the soul, therefore if you don't use your eyes to communicate, it can severely restrict the communication process, having an effect not just on the range of your voice and the content of your speech, but on your very integrity.

Learn to activate your eyes, using different levels of focus and brightness, opening your eyes more or less and moving your eyebrows up and down.

BRIGHT, OPEN EYES

Try opening your eyes really wide and notice how your eyebrows will automatically rise up with them. This can show a sense of excitement or wonder. Or you can use your eyebrows and wide eyes to highlight different words in your sentence.

If you use this bright, open-eye position when greeting someone – let's say, meeting someone for the first time – it will make a very different impression than if you simply keep your eyes still and smile with your mouth. Try it now in front of a mirror. Simply say 'Hi' in two ways: one with your eyes wide open and your eyebrows coming up (and a smile) and the other with your eyes still and a smile. You should see and feel a difference.

The first way makes a statement to the person you are meeting: 'I am genuinely delighted to meet you.' The second says: 'I'm reserved. I'm not yet sure if I am pleased to meet you or not.'

Do be careful, though, of overdoing it, which will not strengthen the effect but rather make you look a bit overexcited!.

Reserved eyes look withdrawn and won't make you want to smile!

Figure 8.1

Confident eyes give a warm expression that can provoke an intuitive smiling response

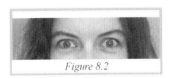

Figure 8.2

Over the top eyes look as though the person is shocked or scared, or even play acting!

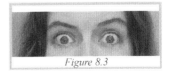

Figure 8.3

LSW Gem: Active eyes and meeting people

There are several different styles of body language that can be used when meeting new people. Many people use a reserved nod, for example. This can work brilliantly for showing status. However, when it comes to engaging, it is less effective and can be intimidating, while active eyes make people feel safe and help them warm to you more easily.

There isn't a 'one size fits all' solution. However, the more you understand your own instrument, and the more notes you can play on it, with an awareness of their effect, the more power you will have.

BRIGHT EYES VERSUS DULL EYES

Bright eyes tend to show an active engagement, a vibrant connection with what you are saying. They can also show sincerity. If you are prepared to look directly at someone and widen your eyes, it can be as if you are allowing them to see into your thoughts.

To achieve this, simply open your eyes a little wider than usual (not as much as the previous position) and think of a little smile and letting that warmth hit your eyes. You can also intensify your gaze. These eyes say 'I'm engaged, alert and pleased to be here'. The effect? Well, often the listener or audience will be pleased too. Brightness is contagious.

Dull eyes, on the other hand, can be more hard work for the listener. The person has hidden themselves away, their soul is inside, not wanting to be seen. You can't tell what is going on in their head, just that they are not altogether engaged. Dull or hooded eyes can give the impression that your mind is elsewhere, or you are tired, bored or worried.

DID YOU KNOW?

Be careful where you look

The direction our eyes look in has been proved to be a lot more relevant than we think. Look at the details below to find out what each directional glance may mean about your thoughts.

Looking up and to the left: Known as visual construction, this indicates that the person is accessing information from their imagination, so a person might do this if you ask about their dream holiday. It also means they could be making up their answer, so if you suspect someone is lying, look to see if their eyes are going up and to the left.

Looking up and to the right: Visual remembering is when we are actually accessing a memory and picturing it in our minds. If you ask someone what their new sofa looks like, they will probably use visual remembering.

Looking middle and to the left: Known as auditory construction, this is where our eyes might go if we are constructing a sound in our mind. If you ask a friend to think of what their voice will sound like when they are 80 years old, they will more than likely look in this direction.

Looking middle and to the right: Auditory remembering indicates where our eyes might go if we are remembering a sound that we have heard before. For example, ask a friend what their partner sounds like and they will more than likely look in this direction.

Looking down and to the left: Kinesthetic direction is the way our eyes might go if we are accessing our actual feelings about something. For example, if you ask a friend about their feelings on the issues of capital punishment, their eyes might go in this direction.

Looking down and to the right: Auditory digital indicates the direction our eyes might go when we are talking to ourselves in our heads. So if you see someone looking in this direction, chances are they are having a conversation with themselves.[2]

Reading eyes exercise...

Let's look at two pictures showing two examples of eyes. Hooded and withdrawn versus wide and open.

Ask yourself the following questions to see the impact our eyes have:

- Who seems more engaged and connected to what they are saying or listening to?
- Who would you describe as having a larger need to share what they are saying?
- Who looks like they would be more interesting and fun company in this particular moment?

Figure 8.4

Example of bright eyes

Figure 8.5

Example of dull eyes

Case study: Using your eyes to express yourself

One of my clients had a particular and rather dramatic shift through the exercise you will do next. He came to me as an intelligent, successful and ambitious City professional. However, he had confidence issues. For years he had believed that he just wasn't a good communicator (it emerged this was baggage left over from childhood) and this had made him withdraw and speak less as a result. When he did speak, it was with restraint.

After our first session, he had made good progress; in part through the techniques we worked on and in part through us bringing to the fore the baggage he had carried around about being a bad communicator. However, the real shift happened in the second session. I had asked him to prepare a piece on what he wanted to achieve in five years' time. He read out what he had prepared, soullessly, looking at the tape recorder the whole time. When he was done, I asked him how it felt. 'Awful,' he replied. 'I felt like there was all this stuff inside me, but I wasn't letting it out into the words.' That was exactly how I had felt watching him. That there was a gulf between this young man and the persona he was prepared to share with the world.

I decided if I could get him to reveal some of his true self, then it would build a bridge to his expression on the inside. That's exactly what happened.

After showing him an example, I asked him to describe a picture in two ways, first with his eyes mask-like, then with his eyes animated. The first time, as expected, by not using his eyes, the impression he gave was that of an automaton, that he didn't care who he was talking to; he didn't feel anything. In the second, animated version, where he gave his eyes and face permission to move along with his descriptions, the answers were quite the opposite.

In giving himself permission to use his eyes, something rather magical happened – he came out of himself. We had quite simply built the bridge. Then I asked him to let me keep the camera rolling while he stood and told me about his five-year mission. The effect was extraordinary. He blossomed, and seemed to delight in communication, his face and eyes were active, he smiled lots, and what's more, his content changed. Where before it had been off the page, now he found charming metaphors to illustrate his points.

When we watched it back on film, it was incredibly moving, as he was vibrant and present on camera. By allowing his outside to be engaged, he had given permission, almost on a subconscious level, for his inner character to step into the room.

The case study above gives an indication of just how powerful the next exercise is. The exercise will help you to become more alive and expressive, so you can bring more of yourself to the table when you speak.

Facial activation exercise...

You will need a camera, web cam or smartphone and a friend or an imaginary person to talk to.

Spend a moment really looking at the picture below, noticing its co-lours, how it feels, the energy of it.

Figure 8.6
A classic painting

Step one

With your eyes and face like a mask, describe the painting out loud – either to someone else or into the camera. Do not let your eyes move at all. You can mention any of the following:

- How it makes you feel.
- The colours and textures.
- A description of what you see.
- Whether you like the picture or not.

Step two

The second time, let your eyes join in as you describe the colours, dimensions and shape of the picture.

Self-observation

- How did you feel when doing the first description?
- How did you feel when doing the second description?
- Did you say anything different the second time round?
- Did you notice a difference in vocal quality?

People often find that letting their eyes join in frees up communication: it gets more exciting, and all of a sudden there is more to say. This is because our bodies are an important part of the communication process. In fact, the more they are allowed to be an extension of our communication, the more expressive we can be.

Eye tennis exercise...

If you really struggle with activating your eyes, this exercise will help you free up your face. This exercise is a little odd-ball (excuse the pun), but it's well worth the effort, as it will help you to use your entire face more. It is better played with another person, probably a child under five!

You are playing imaginary tennis with your partner. However, rather than holding an imaginary racket, the ball is responsive to your eye movements.

Now play, sending the ball around the court for your partner to grab and hit back with their eyes.

> **Send it high and to the right.**

> **Send it speedily over the net.**

> **Bounce it.**

> **Lose it in a bush and scrunch up your eyes to find it and get it back.**

This is really to get you used to using the muscles around your eyes a little more, scrunching up your face, lifting your eyebrows.

This game may feel silly, and indeed, I found it amusing when I played it with clients, but it's hugely useful in isolating and beginning to develop that part of your body.

LSW Gem: Active eyes and emphasis

One very simple trick to make your communication more engaging is to use 'active eyes' to add emphasis to the important words in your sentence. Like a facial highlighter, you can widen your eyes over the important words. The effect this has is twofold:

1. It draws your listener's attention directly to that word, making sure the meaning and the impact go right in (placing the idea in their mind again).

2. It pushes you to slow down a little over that word and become more conscious of both saying it and its impact which, in turn, makes it more effective.

This is a particularly useful device if you are a non-native speaker and find people sometimes misunderstand you. Everyone recognises the 'eye language' and that will help signpost what's important for your listener so they can (if necessary) spend some extra processing time registering those words.

Begin to notice in your next interactions, and when watching people on TV, how much eye movement there is. Notice where you are on the scale, and also what you like and what feels comfortable.

The first step of this process is simply bringing it to conscious awareness. The second is starting to try things out. Don't worry – it may take a while before using active eyes starts to feel natural – particularly if you are not someone who is used to being expressive. You will need to find your new comfort zone and be aware that whatever that is (and that's up to you to decide), it's unlikely to feel totally comfortable at the beginning. The best thing to do is to add little moments in to your everyday life, and be sensitive as to how you feel and the reactions you receive. You can also practise by doing the eye ball exercise, and film yourself as much as possible doing the first descriptive exercise. The more you can see and feel the difference, the more confidence you will have with bringing your new alive face into the public domain.

If you really go for it, it takes between 21 and 28 days to form a habit. Practise every day for three weeks, and it becomes your way of doing things. Change is possible.

Just Smile

A happy bedfellow of active eyes is the smile. A genuine smile can, as the cliché goes, light up a room. It certainly can light up a face and make any person look beautiful in the space of a second. If you can use your smile to make a first impression on someone, you will be surprised by its power. But the smile has to be genuine to be effective.

Figure 8.7

Unsmiling

Figure 8.8

Smiling

See how the smile lights up the face in the pictures above?

A DUCHENNE SMILE

A genuine smile is spontaneous and it is the smile that best demonstrates satisfaction or happiness. This is the smile that reaches your eyes – and that's how you know it is genuine. A really genuine smile actually has its own name. It's called the Duchenne smile and it activates 36 muscles.

DID YOU KNOW?

THE SCIENCE OF A SMILE

When you smile a genuine smile, your eyes will also appear half shut. This is because at the final stage of the smile, the muscles around the eyes, called the orbicular muscles, contract. This 'half shut' look is actually a muscular trigger that activates centres in the brain which regulate the production of pleasant emotions. Which is why they say genuine smiles release endorphins. It also means that if you don't see the half-shut eyes that come at the end of a smile, the smile is likely to be without genuine joy from the person who gives it.[3]

A genuine smile is linked to the part in our brain that manages our pleasant emotions, suggesting that not only do we smile genuinely when we feel good, but also a genuine smile can make us feel good. And indeed this is a known fact. Smile broadly now for ten seconds and happy endorphins will be released. You may find it's in the form of amusement when you finally release the rictus grin, but those are the endorphins taking action! Another interesting experiment: smile the same broad smile (go on, as broad as you can) and try and think of something negative while you are doing it.

I'll bet you can't!

This fits nicely with some other studies linking smiles to both a happier and longer life like this interesting study described below.

DID YOU KNOW?

Smiling and its proven link to wellbeing

In the longitudinal study of Mills College graduates, Keltner and colleague LeeAnne Harker coded the smiles of 114 women who had their university yearbook photo taken sometime during 1958 and 1960. All but three of the young women smiled. However, 50 had Duchenne smiles and 61 had non-Duchenne, courtesy, smiles.

The genuine smile group were more likely to get and stay married, and had higher score evaluations of physical and emotional wellbeing. Remarkably, Keltner's study was able to find this connection more than 30 years after the college photos were taken. [4]

So getting into the habit of smiling in a way that spreads across your whole face is a positive thing from more than one perspective!

Research also shows that genuine smiles lead to more positive social interactions. Below is a study that adds some scientific support to this. It describes how people anticipate a genuine smile and tend to respond with the same.

DID YOU KNOW?

A genuine smile begets… a genuine smile

Heerey, a psychologist from Bangor University, differentiates between polite smiles – which occur as a result of a social norm dictating it's an appropriate time to smile – and genuine smiles, which signify pleasure, occur spontaneously, and are indicated by engagement of specific muscles around the eyes. As such, she sees genuine smiles as a form of social reward. Heerey was interested to see the extent to which people anticipate a genuine smile, because of its greater value, and she found that, in fact, they did.

An observational study showed pairs of strangers getting to know one another. When they exchanged smiles, they almost always matched the particular smile type, whether genuine or polite.

However, more intriguing was the lab-based studies. Data from electrical sensors on participants' faces revealed that they engaged smile-related muscles when they expected a genuine smile to appear but showed no such activity when expecting polite smiles.[4]

Case study: A smile is infectious

Many years ago, when I was still at university, I used to do promotional work as a summer job. As I was interested in psychology, I found it a fascinating way to learn about people en masse, while earning some much-needed cash. There was one particular day that moved me deeply and has always stayed in my memory. I was giving out flyers in the City of London; it was the end of a long day and I was flagging. So I decided to start smiling real genuine smiles at people. Keep in mind this was the end of a long day for them, too, so my expectations of what I would get back were pretty low. But instead something magical happened.

As I looked at a person and genuinely smiled, almost all the people I smiled at began smiling at me too. Real, proper smiles. This made me even happier, so I was broadly smiling, which must have been infectious, as more and more people smiled broadly back at me. I was so moved by this, I welled up. As I told friends later, I had learnt something huge that day. That everyone – even the most seemingly surly of people – has a smile inside them. You just need to release it. And the best way to release it? With a genuine smile.

Recognising a duchenne smile exercise...

Have a look at the pictures below. You will notice the genuine smiles from a really instinctive place. They will probably make you want to smile, too. That is the 'currency' the psychologist Heerey was talking about.

Duchenne or not Duchenne?

Take a look at the smiles below and answer the following questions for each pair of photos:

- Who would you prefer to sit next to at a dinner party, the person in column A or B?

- If you were told one of the pair is being paid to be with you, and the other genuinely liked you, which one would you think has been paid?

- Who do you think will be more fun?

- Who do you think is happier?

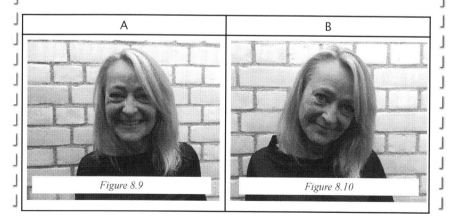

A	B
Figure 8.9	Figure 8.10

Figure 8.11

Figure 8.12

Figure 8.13

Figure 8.14

Figure 8.15

Figure 8.16

Figure 8.17   Figure 8.18

You may notice that the last two pictures are really difficult to distinguish from each other. But just ask the last question – who do you think is happier? – and you should know in a shot.

WHAT DOES THIS TELL US?

I imagine most of the time your answers will lean towards the person with the Duchenne smile being the one who you find more authentic, who you think is more fun and who you would rather sit next to at a dinner party. Not only do we have an automatic instinct about Duchenne smiles but we also have an automatic response: we like them more, we want to spend more time with them, we trust their motives, we think they are happy. So if you are thinking that about others, chances are they are thinking it about you. A good case for becoming a genuine smiler!

HOW TO SMILE A GENUINE SMILE

For the smilers reading this, you don't need any guidance. For others, if you think you rarely smile, and adding some warmth to your facial expressions could really lift your communication, then try the exercise below.

Duchenne smiling exercise...

First, try the non-genuine smile. Paste a smile onto your face (literally just turning up the sides of your mouth). Don't let it hit your eyes. Hold for five seconds. Be aware of how this feels.

Now for the genuine smile. Think of something lovely, like sinking in to a warm bath after a hard day, or an extremely cute kitten, or look at the picture of the baby below. Let the warmth of the image start at your eyes, and let your eyes crinkle as a result. Allow the corners of your mouth to turn upwards, then keep on going. Hold this, go bigger, multiply it, let your eyes become warmer, as if they are filled with joy. Be aware of how this feels.

Figure 8.19

This kind of smile that allows warmth to spread across your face is your currency. This smile can build connections and send positive messages to others.

How smiling changes meaning exercise...

1.   **Start with your genuine smile.**

2.   **Now say the following lines:**

-    What a beautiful day.

-    The report you wrote is really good.

-    I'm impressed.

3.   **Now say the lines with a straight face, be sincere and focused.**

4.   **Now answer the following questions:**

-    How did the facial expression affect the quality of the message?

-    Did you find a smile suited some phrases more than others?

-    You might have felt that smiling was great for rapport, and less good for authority and impact. You might have noticed that the quality of your voice changes. That's because a smile also changes the shape of your vocal cavity, so you can literally hear if someone is smiling.

If you want to reassure an anxious employee that they are doing well you might want to go for the more impactful straight face. If you want to build rapport with a nervous new intern, you would probably rather go for the warm smile. Also be aware of how the sentence changes its meaning and intention with and without a smile.

Genuine smiles are good for engagement and rapport building. They are also powerful for walking into a room and making an instant positive impression. Some people make tactical decisions not to smile, feeling that it decreases authority and may mean you are not taken seriously. This is not necessarily the case, but each person must decide what is right for them. As with everything in this book, there is no right way. But there are tools and choices. If you have the tools, you can have the choice, and understand their impact.

Other Facial Expressions

According to various studies, there are seven types of facial expressions which are universal across all cultures. Charles Darwin (1809–1882) was the first to suggest that they were universal and since then, hundreds of studies have supported this idea. They are joy, anger, contempt, surprise, sadness, disgust and fear, each with its relevant combination of mouth, eyebrow and eye positions.

Useful for communication? Yes. You need to know what your face is saying. If your face is set in an angry scowl, then it will be useful to know that is what people are reading, not just culturally, but innately. As such, if you don't want them to think you are angry, it will be useful to learn to change it.

Contempt

Surprise

Joy

Anger

Disgust

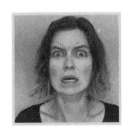

Fear

Sadness

Facial expression to influence and captivate
/ GOLDEN RULES /

1. Use your eyes to add life to your speech, and notice how people respond with more attention and it's easier to engage.

2. If you are tired, push yourself to engage your eyes and face to achieve a better connection.

3. Smiling is great for making a positive first impression and for rapport building.

4. Smiling is a choice, not necessarily suited to all situations or people, but you can always make your eyes warm and alive even if you don't want to smile.

5. Smiling has strong biological triggers in both the smiler and the receiver, and is therefore a powerful communication tool.

Chapter 9 | The true art of listening |

In this chapter you will learn about:

- **Making the speaker feel important:** Avoid feeding your own ego.

- **Three levels of listening:** And how to tune in to the speaker

- **Active listening:** And how to do it

- **How to ask good questions:** The value of drawing people out

- **How to build rapport on the phone:** You can communicate through your voice

- **How to charm:** A skill you'll never regret learning

Communication is a two-way process, so this chapter is dedicated to listening, and perhaps a new concept to most: three-level listening. It was revelatory to me when I started to do it, so I hope it is for you, too. To show how effective it can be, we spotlight Bill Clinton and why his listening made him, according to some, such a powerful and well-liked president.

WHY IS IT YOU WOULD WANT to tell a particular person a story and not someone else? Why do you find someone charming at a party? Why do you enjoy speaking to one person more than another? It is because they make you feel good. They demonstrate that they are interested in you, through their bodies, voices and words. They have the gift of making you feel like you are the most important person in the room. That's why we like talking to them.

The most effective way to build rapport is to make the other person feel important. There are a few ways to do this, and we will explore each of them in this chapter. Firstly, it starts with an attitude. We can't really make someone feel important if we don't feel it. Next it's about the quality of our listening. It's important to attend fully to the person we are listening to, rather than, as many of us are prone to do, only half listen, or think about ourselves. This is explored using a coaching tool of three levels of listening. Next we need to show the speaker we are listening and interested, and this is about non-verbal communication (called active listening) and the questions we ask. All of these are skills that can be learned.

Making The Speaker Feel Important

According to Les Giblin in his book *Crucial Conversations*, making someone feel important fosters mutual respect. He outlines three steps to making people feel important. These are simple and full of impact.

BELIEVING SOMEONE IS IMPORTANT

You can't make anyone feel important if secretly you think they are insignificant. According to Giblin, you can tune in to someone's importance by recognising the uniqueness and complexity of each individual. The more we appreciate the unique mental life of someone, the more we can step into each exchange with a genuine curiosity and interest in what makes them tick. Les says the people who have the most influence are the ones who believe in the importance of others.

NOTICE OTHER PEOPLE

The second step is to notice other people. People love to feel noticed. There have been numerous studies on what gets people to work harder or be more motivated. It's about being interested in them.

DON'T ACT SUPERIOR

We are all driven by egos, and we all like to feel important. This is natural, and yet we can get caught in a need to show ourselves to be important to others. This can lead to us listening with self-interest, waiting for the opportunity to share our story or a time when we did it better. Giblin draws an interesting comparison with feeding the ego and feeding your stomach. If we have a healthy dose of self-assurance, the equivalent of three meals a day, then we won't be seeing every interaction as a potential opportunity to grab some ego food. If, however, we are underfed, then interactions can easily become an ego-feeding scenario. And yet, interestingly, one of our most effective ways of impressing someone is to let them know we are impressed by them.

LSW Gem: Attitude

The attitude with which you enter a conversation is also very important. If, for example, you go in to a communication situation expecting a person to be warm and honest and open, then chances are they will perform accordingly. If, on the other hand, you expect your listeners to be boring or snobbish, then you are more likely to get the expected response. So checking in with yourself and your attitude before you enter a communication situation is a helpful trick. If you notice a negative thought, try to swap it for a positive. At the very least, put your body and face into a position where you will appear positive. As we know, you can work from the outside in that way, changing how you feel by changing your body language.

Three Levels Of Listening

Good-quality listening is one of the easiest ways to show someone they are important to us, because good listening makes a person feel we are interested in them. We direct our attention to what we value, so when we give another person our attention, it tells them we value them and they are worth our time and energy.

A really good place to look for listening skills is in the fields of coaching and psychotherapy, as they are professionals who are paid to listen and listen well. Fortunately, I have trained in both. One of the most powerful gems I learnt on listening was through my coaching training and it describes three levels of listening. As a listener, when we are wanting to make people feel important, we want to be listening at levels two and three. When we are listening at level one, it is ego listening.

The good news is, once you become aware of the three levels, you can catch yourself at level-one listening and move quickly out of it and tune in to the speaker again, which is why it is such a great tool. When I fully absorbed it, it shifted the quality of my coaching to a more powerful level. I spent a lot of time listening in level three, where you become attuned to the nuance of the speaker's physicality and tone, even to their breathing. I found listening from this place enabled me to help the client so much more, as I was able to reflect back what was going on for them.

LEVEL-ONE LISTENING

The first level is listening to someone with ourselves in the forefront of our minds – so when the speaker says something, we think about how it relates to us. Someone tells a story and we think of a similar story. Someone puts themselves down and we tell ourselves how great we are. Someone finds something effortless and we think how difficult we find it. Level-one listening is essentially from the ego. It might be to berate or promote oneself, but it is always self-orientated. It is fine in certain circumstances, and a lot of listening is done here. For rapport-building it can work well, to share similar stories and experiences, but it's important to remember to acknowledge the other person from this level, or the speaker can feel quite ignored.

LEVEL-TWO LISTENING

This is when you listen to the speaker's words and see links between their words and other things they have said or done in previous conversations. You're developing an analytical understanding of the person and getting curious about them. This is great because it is really attending to them. It can be as simple as just enjoying what they share, laughing along with them and commenting on how funny they are, or agreeing with them. It's really about the individual you are speaking to.

LEVEL-THREE LISTENING

This is listening with your body rather than with your brain (level two) or with your ego (level one). When you listen from here, you drop down into your body and become like a listening instrument. From this place, it feels like you've switched off your brain a bit, and you let the words wash over you to some extent. Instead, you are listening to their breath, their tone of voice, the speed at which they speak, their enthusiasm levels. If you are with them (although this is also very effective on the phone) you can take notice of their posture and their body language, their facial expression and level of eye contact.

You are also listening for your own feelings about it. So rather than see a person with their arms crossed and think, that means they are being defensive, you tune in to your own body and see what you feel about it. From this place, your body and feelings might well be giving you lots of information about where they are at. If, for example, you notice your own breath is quick and you feel uncomfortable, chances are they feel uncomfortable too. By tuning into your level-three reading of a situation, you can bring in an intuitive layer to your relationships which will serve you incredibly well.

EXAMPLE OF THREE LEVELS OF LISTENING

Below is a chart that gives an example of a listener's head narrative at each level of listening.

Speaker says	Level-one listening	Level-two listening	Level-three listening
I'm terrible at team sports. I'm always last to be picked for the team. It's awful.	How awful. Thank God I'm never last to be picked. I couldn't handle that.	She says she's terrible, but she repeatedly puts herself in team sport situations. I wonder why.	Her breathing is fast, she said awful with lots of energy, she seems distressed. Wonder what 'awful' means to her.
My new boyfriend finally invited me on holiday!	My boyfriend hasn't taken me on holiday for over a year.	New and finally – hmmm that's an interesting insight. Perhaps a holiday is some kind of marker. Wonder how that works for her.	She seems so happy. Her voice is light and joyful.
I have been thinking about why I always get told off by my boss, and I think it's because she's jealous of me	Typical – she's so big-headed. When my boss gets angry with me, I actually take responsibility.	I wonder what she gets told off about, and what makes her think it's jealousy.	She sounds like she is trying to get to grips with this. Her voice is quite small, and I get the sense this has hurt her more than she is letting on.

Three-level listening exercise...

Next time you are speaking to someone, see if you can make the shift to level-two and then level-three listening. Move from the thoughts in your head to how you feel, and ask yourself: what is the person saying beneath their words? What is their mood? You will be surprised by how much new information you get. And the more you practise, the easier and more natural this skill becomes.

SPOTLIGHT BILL CLINTON

An example of an amazing listener

An interesting article from the Huffington Post, entitled 'Bill Clinton has a superpower, and mastering it can make you successful beyond belief' states that Clinton's secret is that he gives everyone he meets his full, undivided attention. Below is an extract.[6]

During a 1992 presidential debate, Clinton and George H W Bush were asked how the national debt affected them personally – and the way the two politicians answered provided a whole lot of insight into their personalities.

While Bush twisted the question to take the focus off himself, before muttering his way through an explanation of how price hikes 'affect everyone', Clinton walked over to the woman who asked the question, looked her in the eye, and asked her how the debt affected her. He explained how, as the governor of Arkansas, he'd seen the people in his state suffer, and how much of an impact it had on him.

In my state, when people lose their jobs, there's a good chance I'll know them by name,

Clinton said.

People can tell when you're actually listening to them – and they love it. It seems simple and obvious, but Clinton built a career on doing what most politicians can't or won't do: connect with ordinary people, look them in the eye and listen to what they have to say. His ability to listen was instrumental in his ability to win people over.

All my life I've been interested in other people's stories,

Clinton wrote in *My Life*.

I wanted to know them, understand them, feel them.

Another article shows the quality of his listening was also in his non-verbal communication.

Clinton looked me in the eyes and seemed to have a genuine interest in what I was saying. His gaze never left me. He made me feel like the most important person in the room at the time, and Microsoft founder Bill Gates was standing right next to us!

Taken from Why Leadership Means Listening by Carmine Gallo

Active Listening

When someone actively listens, they are giving lots of non-verbal signals that they are interested in what the speaker is saying. Eye contact, smiles, open body language, small filler sounds – all of these make up active listening. If none of those is present, then it can get pretty uncomfortable. However, if you actively listen to someone, you will find that they will give you more detail and become more receptive to what you then have to say. You will also find that it is far easier to flow into a conversation, as the two of you build a comfortable rapport.

EYE CONTACT

This is about having your eyes on the speaker and being alert to them. Don't multi-task or put your attention (and perception) elsewhere. For the speaker, when the listener looks away, it is very noticeable. It also usually leads to a drop in confidence for the speaker, as they make the assumption that the listener isn't interested. If you continue not to look at the speaker, eventually most speakers will shorten what they are saying or dry up. It's a huge communication skill to be good at drawing people out – and much of that is about eye contact and building rapport.

ACTIVE EYES

Allow your eyes to respond to what the speaker is saying. Let your eyebrows move, your eyes be alert, and open them wider if you hear something particularly interesting or surprising. Don't allow your eyes to be vacant, stare at the middle distance or switch off. The person speaking can tell instantly, and it is one sure way to break rapport. It is the listener's responsibility to keep eye contact on the speaker. It's the speaker's responsibility to break it every so often so it doesn't become a staring match.

NODS AND OPEN BODY LANGUAGE

Nodding is a great way to build rapport and state without interrupting that you are listening to what someone is saying and are very much with them. Couple the nod with a slight smile or lift of the eyes for even more powerful rapport-building. Face the individual where possible with your body, which will make them feel they have your full attention (it is fine for your legs to be pointed in a different direction, as long as your torso is facing them). Don't cross your arms or slump and round your shoulders.

SOUNDS AND WORDS

Using little affirmative sounds creates a background rapport-building melody which shows the listener you really are engaged. Using tone and colour in your voice is a great way of showing interest. If this isn't your norm it might feel a bit odd at first, but you will soon find it comes naturally. This is also really useful on the phone where you don't have eye contact, and can show someone that you are with them and interested in them by using encouraging sounds. Good sounds to use are 'uh huh', 'yeah', 'really', 'ahh', 'great', 'good', 'mmm', etc.

It's also useful to paraphrase back what you are hearing at some points, or to make a little affirmative comment.

Effective listening exercise...

Imagine you are telling a story about a funny event that happened at work. Your listeners are either A, B, C or D. Ask yourself the following:

- Look at the pictures, who would you rather tell your story to?
- Your story has a short two-minute version or a longer ten-minute version. Which version would you choose to tell A, B, C and D?
- Who do you feel more confident and interesting with?

A

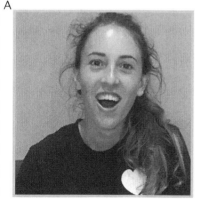

B

I think you've probably got the point! If you were being listened to by anyone in the first two pictures you'd feel pretty good about telling them more, right?

And if it was someone from the last two pictures, the chances are you'd want to have your story finished as soon as possible to get the pain over. If someone was listening to you like that, you'd be forgiven for thinking you must be incredibly boring! If you tend to listen as if you were in the last two pictures, then think of this. You may be doing excellent level-two or three listening but the person you are listening to won't know it and it will affect how much they want to share. Keep this in mind next time you are listening and adjust your face accordingly. If you want them to share less, then framing a face like the last two pictures can be a good tactic to achieve that!

LSW Gem: The power of active listening

We do an exercise at LSW where the listener asks the speaker a number of mundane questions, such as their age and full name. The first time they ask actively, with bright smiley eyes, nods, and little interested comments. The speaker - unsure of what the exercise is - begins to warm up. Very soon it's like a conversation, and the speaker is chatting away, answering quite private questions - like 'do you get on with your siblings?' - with ease.

Then we get the same people to do exactly the same exercise, but this time the listener is asked to listen inactively. They don't smile, they cross their arms, and barely look at the speaker. The conversation, as you can imagine, is a whole lot shorter.

The speaker gives the bare minimum of details, and later describes wanting to get it over with as soon as possible.

It's a fantastic exercise to get everybody to see how accessible both ways are, anyone can actively or non-actively listen, and the effects are huge.

Active listening

Body language: open	Verbal language: soft, fillers	Tone of voice
Open gestures	Okay	Warm
Smiles	Sure	Low
Warm eyes	I understand	Soft and slow
Nods	I see where you are coming from	From the diaphragm
Mirroring the speaker's body language		Bright and chirpy
Relaxed	Great	
	Ahh	
	Mmmm	

Non-active listening

Body language: closed	Verbal language: negative, direct	Tone of voice
Closed	No	Sharp
Crossed arms	You've got it wrong	Monotone
Body turned away	I disagree	Quick and clipped
No smiles	You statements: You said... you did	From the throat
Unmoving eyes	Factual statements: That's not the case... That's rubbish...	
Avoidance of eye contact	Silence	

LSW Gem: What to do if you are speaking to an inactive listener

We all know how disheartening it can be if you are speaking to someone who has no listening skills. It can feel like you want to just stop talking then and there. However, you do have some options - two in fact. You can give up, or you can keep going.

If the situation is important and the message close to your heart, then you might as well keep imagining that they are about ten times more interested than they make out, and throw your new-found techniques into the communication. Because one thing is for certain, you are never going to get close to engaging disengaged listeners without effort. And with effort, you just might do it. So if someone inactively listens, try telling yourself they simply lack the skill, and go for it. Up a gear or two and see what happens!

Top Tips:

- When you are listening actively, your mind gets active too. More questions are generated and you become curious, which often leads to buzzier conversations, with more energy and connection. Win-win really.

- You can try mirroring the body language of the person you are speaking to.

- Don't multi-task – focus on your speaker closely.

How To Ask Good Questions

Questions are incredibly powerful in terms of building rapport because a genuine question requires an answer from the other person, which creates an immediate connection.

A question says: 'I want to know what you think' or 'I want to know more about you'. This is why open questions can be more powerful than closed questions, because you are asking for more detail and information from the other person.

'Do you like football?' is a closed question, requiring a yes or no answer. It says you have a limited interest in the response. In contrast, 'What do you think about football?' says that you want to know about the other person, their thoughts, opinions and how their mind works.

Asking questions is an equalising of status. For the person being asked a question, it makes them feel that they are important.

THE THREE TYPES OF QUESTION

Open questions: These require more than one-word answers. They leave the individual space to talk. They begin or include words like how, what or why.

- What kind of sport do you like?
- How do you know about psychology?
- Why are you interested in Impressionism?

Focused or yes/no questions: These get to the nitty-gritty of it. They usually require a single-word answer or a simple phrase. They begin with words like do you, are you, will you. They can often end the conversation.

- Do you play sport?
- Do you like prawns?
- Are you happy?

Paraphrasing questions: These help to make sure you understood correctly. They are about repeating back the idea to the speaker. These are very powerful in terms of showing you have understood or been listening and that you are with the speaker. Therapists use these types of questions a lot. It shows that you are listening and also encourages the speaker to open up more about the topic.

- So you said you love all sports, except for water sports?

You can also a version of paraphrasing if you are doing level-three listening, where you pick one word or phrase that stood out because of how they said it, and just ask more about it. Because you are listening in level three, you will probably not have any ideas about what they mean, but you will be surprised by how much they open up.

- You said the word 'awful' with a lot of weight behind it – what's that about?

How To Build Rapport On The Phone

On the phone, your voice is all you have to make that all-important impression, so it's vital that – if the call matters – you create the situation that will allow you to be at your best.

POSITION

Your listener may not be able to see your body, but your position matters. If you are tangled up in a folded position, if your shoulders are hunched or your arms crossed, all of this will affect your voice. Your breath will not be grounded (bad posture means you can't reach your diaphragm) and your voice will probably sound more strained. If your body is folded, it will add tension to your voice, thinning it out. So sit comfortably, body relaxed, with a straight spine so you can take deep breaths.

ATTENTION

People can hear when your attention is elsewhere. It is so easy to get caught up in doing more than one thing at once, but if the call is important, just don't multi-task. Giving someone your full attention on an important call is crucial to having a productive conversation. People can hear in your voice when you are only half present, and most people will start to shut down in some way at that point. Not only that, you can miss subtle shifts in their voice, or even whole sentences.

Think of one of those beautiful and sensitive ferns that clamps shut as soon as it is touched. One drop of inattention can have the same effect as a touch on the fern, and you can lose the person on the other end of the line. Yes, you can coax them back out, but who knows the damage done? So if it's important, give your full attention.

ATTITUDE AND ENVIRONMENT

Make sure that you are in the right head space for this call. If it's important, don't take the call walking down the street. Give yourself all you need to perform brilliantly. You have only your voice and your mind so you will need to concentrate that bit more to make sure you get the outcome you want.

One nice little trick is to consciously step into a different zone, a zone where you are the professional, as if you were entering into an important meeting with only that person.

I used to coach clients on the phone, and I would step into that call ensuring there were no distractions, no external thoughts that could leap in at me, and I would treat it like an important meeting with just that person. From that place I could hear every nuance in their speech, every shift in their energy. I was so tuned in I could hear a wave of sadness or excitement pass through them without any sound to indicate its presence. The power of that total attention for the client allowed for huge shifts to happen for them.

It might be that your phone conversations demand a different kind of energy. Whichever it is, think about it, be conscious of your own objective and step into it with focus. You'll be amazed at how much more effective phone conversations can be.

SMILE ON THE PHONE

People can hear a smile in your voice. If when someone calls, you sound happy to hear from them, it creates the fertile soil of receptivity. If, on the other hand, you sound disappointed to hear from them, then the whole conversation is back-footed. And these are not things people consciously hear, they just feel it, so they may feel happy and not be sure why, or they may feel disappointed or slightly rejected or unwanted and they are not sure why. Those initial feelings can have an enormous effect on the outcome of a conversation.

Think about it this way. If you are starting on a walk and you turn a fraction to your right and start walking, in half an hour you will be in a very different place than you would be if you walked straight ahead.

It's the same with that first impression. So smile and make them feel warm and see where it takes you!

IN TERMS OF YOUR TONE

Be aware of your tone on the phone. For women, a higher tone is more informal and girly, a lower tone is more professional and authoritative. When I speak to clients or anyone in a more formal setting, my voice naturally goes to a lower tone and as such sounds more authoritative. It's not something I do consciously, but I am aware of it and how well it works. Similarly, a man with a higher-pitched voice will be less likely to be taken seriously in a work setting, so learning to adjust the pitch of your voice to suit the environment is definitely a bonus. For more on this, please look at Chapter 18.

How To Charm

As with all communication, we are looking at the three main categories of your voice, your body and your content. Unsurprisingly, all three are of huge importance when it comes to being charming.

VOICE AND TONE

If you sound happy to hear from someone or show that you are happy to see them, then this is the first crucial point of charm. Fill your voice with warmth. Let it be like honey, not vinegar. Think warm and golden, not sharp and acidic.

BODY AND EYES

Let your eyes and voice light up, let a smile light up your face, and make that smile especially for them, and you already have an advantage on most. Your body language should be open and relaxed, no crossed arms here. Let your position be a gentle mirror of theirs if you want to really build rapport. Let your eyes be bright and engaged, make good eye contact, and let your gaze be sincere but gentle.

CONTENT

Now for your words. Show interest in them. I repeat, whoever they are, if you want to charm them, show interest. That's your fertile soil. Don't say 'hello', say 'how are you?' in a way that shows you are genuinely interested or happy to see them. Follow that with another question, a genuine question, that shows engagement and interest.

MAKE THEM FEEL SPECIAL

Depending on what you want from the communication, you will either work on building more rapport, or speak. Whatever it is you want, make it special. Let them blossom and flourish under the warm gaze of your attention. Smile. They are charming. Actively listen. They are interesting. If you make them feel special, then you're half way there.

Quick Steps To Being Charming

- Happy to see them from the twinkling eyes to the Duchenne smile.

- Open body language.

- Warm voice, slow expressive tones.

- Genuine interest.

- Genuine acknowledgement if appropriate.

- Ask and see what happens.

Case study: Be first in line

When I was looking to buy a house, it was in a seller's market, which meant that houses were coming on the market and flying off before anyone even knew they were there. The only way to be in the know was to charm the estate agents, so I set out to do just that. I would use my chirpiest voice, engage them with all my skill, until I had them all calling me telling me about the new arrivals.

One day, I answered the phone without thinking and used a more neutral tone of voice. Immediately the agent asked me I was okay as I didn't sound my usual chirpy self. This estate agent was calling me up to offer me a special first dibs on a new property just on the market. If I answered the phone like that all the time, I can promise you, he would not be calling me first, whether he knew the reason or not.

Make no bones about it, your tone of voice makes a huge difference.

The true art of listening
/ GOLDEN RULES /

1. Be curious about the speaker – see them as genuinely important, get interested in discovering what makes them unique.

2. Actively listening involves head nods, open body language and filler sounds.

3. Learn to listen at level three so you can read the nuances in someone's body.

4. When speaking on the phone, smile, give your full attention and you can change the whole tangent of the call.

5. A warm voice and a genuine smile, plus a simple bit of interest will do wonders on the charm front in most situations.

PART 3

The right tools to use in different situations

Chapter 10 | Find out what makes you tick |

In this chapter you will learn about:

- **Five steps to finding your values:** Know what really matters to you
- **Values in your life:** Applying your values to life decisions

Values are your driving forces, what is important to you. They will come from your culture, your belief systems, your early influences and your education and background. These are the qualities you associate with and are proud of, qualities and ideals you aspire towards. There are no wrong values; all of them are good and clean and equal. So it's really all about what resonates with you.

THIS IS CERTAINLY DEEPER WORK than perhaps you were expecting in a book on communication, and you may feel disconnected from the more day-to-day tools of sounding great and speaking well. However, it is this kind of self-knowledge that, once captured, can sit in the background and infuse and improve everything that you do. You can apply it in every form of communication. It can help you to know why you are giving a presentation, what makes you passionate about working for the company you work for, why and how you need to have a difficult conversation with an unruly team member. And it will give you a real grasp on what drives and inspires you so you can drive and inspire others.

Connect whatever you are saying to your real values, and your audience or listeners will feel it, and it will impact on them as well: it's a whole new level of communication.

Five Steps To Finding Your Values

Try to complete each step in one go and do the whole process either in one sitting or over a few days. Find a quiet space to do the work, and enjoy – you are about to embark on some fantastic self-coaching, to know yourself better and increase your understanding of what makes you tick. Please don't at any point think about 'shoulds'. They are banished from here. Instead look at that which resonates with you, not what you think should resonate, or what people around you want to resonate, but your truth.

STEP ONE: GATHER EXPERIENCES

To begin, write down some examples of the following experiences:

- Describe a time when you were really proud of yourself.
- Describe a person you really admire and the qualities they represent.
- Talk about a peak experience where everything came together and you felt truly happy.
- Describe a time where you were angry.

For example: A Time When I Was Really Proud Of Myself

About 18 months into running London Speech Workshop and after my first teacher dinner. I had about six teachers and my assistant round a table, all sharing their experiences of teaching: what they loved, what was powerful, what suggestions they had for making it better. They all talked with passion and excitement about London Speech Workshop, and I realised I had built something bigger than me. Something that was an entity of its own, that people were proud to be associated with. That felt incredible.

Values associated: Creation, collaboration, inspiration, pioneering, originality, stewardship, excellence, adventure, harmony, leadership, contribution.

STEP TWO: FIND ASSOCIATED VALUES

The next step is to look for the values that emerge in each of the first scenarios. Use the box of suggested values below to give you ideas (although the list is not exhaustive, feel free to add your own) and scoop up as many as feel resonant. There is no number limit for now (whittling down comes later) so have fun!

Examples of values

Accomplishment, accountability, accuracy, achievement, adventure, ambition, arts, beauty, certainty, challenge, collaboration, communication, compassion, competency, competition, contribution, contentment, courage, creativity, credibility, decisiveness, dedication, dependability, dignity, discipline/order, diversity, efficiency, empathy, empowerment, enjoyment, enthusiasm, environment, equality, excellence, faith, fame, family, flexibility, freedom, friendliness, friendships, fun, generosity, gentleness, grace, gratitude, growth, hard work, harmony, helping society, honesty, humility, improvement, independence, individuality, influence, inner harmony, innovation, integrity, intelligence, kindness, learning, love, loyalty, nature, optimism, organization, originality, passion, persistency, physical challenge, quality, reputation, resilience respect, responsibility, security, self awareness, self-respect, service, sharing, status, stewardship, strength, success, teamwork, truth, wisdom.

Top tip: It helps if you detach yourself from the situation and ask yourself what values are obvious here.

STEP THREE: FINDING YOUR VALUES FOR THE TIME WHEN YOU WERE ANGRY

For the angry scenario, it's slightly different. You need to be looking at what made you angry, and find the opposite value of that. For example, I hate bad service at a restaurant. I think it's the laziness and apathy that makes me annoyed. So I look for the opposite of those things, and I get work ethic and passion. See?

STEP FOUR: PICK OUT YOUR TEN MOST RESONANT VALUES

Now you should have a fairly sizeable list of values for each of the questions, so pick out the most resonant values – the ones that really stand out from those you have chosen.

STEP FIVE: CHOOSE YOUR TOP SIX VALUES

List your top six values, then articulate what each one means to you. If choosing one over the other is difficult, don't despair, because when you describe what it means to you, you may find that it encapsulates a lot of the other values. You can change these as you like, but you will find that while some change a little, there are some key ones that describe you and what is important to you.

Congratulations! You have completed your values.

Values In Your Life

Now that you have your core values, you can use them to make decisions about your life. In fact, they can help in every decision you need to make. Do you go to the party or stay in to work? Well, which value is more important to you at that moment?

Connection / adventure? Go to the party! Discipline / success? Stay and work!

See what I mean? In the coaching world, they say that a life lived honouring your values is a life lived fully in resonance. This is a great coaching exercise. Write down your core values and put a number between one and ten on how much you are honouring that value currently in your life. Now pick one of the lower ones and brainstorm some actions you could take which would mean you can honour it more.

If, for example, you have fun and success as two core values, but fun is honoured at 9 and success is being honoured at 4, then you might decide to stay in and work on the project. You might also decide to make some bigger changes to your life.

VALUES AND YOUR WORK

Hopefully, you can find your values in your work. Many people find this exercise really useful in helping them to know why they are doing what they are doing. If you feel your work doesn't reflect your values in any way, then this might be an indicator it's time to change your role or your job. It's very hard to bring your best self to the table, to be a great communicator, to manage well or be a productive employee, if your time is spent in dissonance with your values.

VALUES AND PUBLIC SPEAKING

Whether you are writing a speech or a presentation, finding your values within it is a great way to bring more of you to the table, and bring some heart to what you are saying. It may be just in one line, something you are proud of. But even one line of honesty about why this project or event is important to you on a value level, can have a strong impact on your audience.

VALUES AND CHALLENGING CONVERSATIONS

As you will see in the following chapters, values can be very useful when it comes to having challenging conversations. Not only in understanding and articulating your own frustrations, but also in being empathetic of the other person's position.

If you want to develop this further, consider working with a coach. I love the Coaches Training Institute approach and many of their coaches offer a sample session.

Find out what makes you tick
/ GOLDEN RULES /

1. Values come from your family, your influences, your most deeply held beliefs.

2. When you know your values, they can help guide your decisions, your choices and the way you choose to communicate with others.

3. A life lived honouring your values is a full and happy life.

4. Knowing your values can give you access to your own authenticity in speeches, presentations and all kinds of pressurised situations.

Chapter 11 | How to be efficient and productive in meetings |

In this chapter you will learn about:

- Meetings and how to prepare for them: And the atmosphere we are looking for
- How to listen well in meetings: Applying your listening skills
- How to speak in meetings: Making your voice heard
- Interrupting well: And how to handle being interrupted

We all know what it's like when we can't quite do ourselves justice in a meeting. Meetings are notorious for giving space to the loudest and the brashest, regardless of the quality of their ideas. This means, if we are not among the louder ones, we need strategies to be heard in meetings so we can let our brilliant ideas out. In this chapter, we explore different kinds of meetings, and three areas that are all highly important in meetings. How to listen well, how to speak well and how to interrupt and be interrupted – well!

Scenario

You're in a meeting, ten people are around a table discussing the latest brilliant idea. You have come armed with some thoughts you have been working on, but the voices are so loud and dominant you wonder if you'll ever get to speak. Finally, you muster up the courage to edge your way in. 'I've got an idea.' Everyone turns to face you. You feel yourself going red.

'Okay, what is it?' says your boss. 'Well, it's...' You leaf through your notes, suddenly panicking that maybe you left the sheet at home. You feel yourself going redder. You find it, and read it from the page with a shaking hand. At the end you look up to see people not quite

paying attention. You had hoped to see eyes filled with excitement and buzzing with ideas, but it's the contrary. Three of the ten are lolling back in their chairs, fiddling with their pens, one's got her chin in her hand in a heavy lean on the table. Your boss thanks you, says it's interesting and asks if there are any questions. He is greeted with silence. 'Right,' he says. 'On with the agenda then.'
The buzz starts up in the room and you wish the chair would swallow you up.

Meetings And How To Prepare For Them

MEETINGS AS A BATTLEGROUND

Meetings can be a harsh place where people do their best to take others down. Nails are out and voices are used as weapons. If you enter into this kind of battle, then the only way to come out on top is if you have sharper nails and a louder voice than the others. And even then it's a small victory as there is no team to work with at the end.

MEETINGS AS A MERRY-GO-ROUND

The other kind of dreaded meeting is the circular one that goes on for what seems like hours with nothing established at the end of it. At these meetings, people tend to speak, agree, disagree, say why they disagree, come up with the next point, disagree, explain why they disagree, come back to the first point, etc. These are as frustrating as they are futile. Again, it's often the louder voices that spin that wheel.

MEETING AS A FERTILE GROUND

We like the idea of a meeting in which people feel safe to step in, where collaboration is key and we are supportive of our colleagues as well as feeling supported by them. A meeting where our own ego may be present, but more prevalent are the shared vision and goals for the company or the department, and everyone is keen to do what they can to achieve those goals. People are willing to put their own ideas aside when they hear a better idea more likely to work, and there is a general enthusiasm about the power of the collective, and the possibility that everyone – from the intern to the exec – has something valuable to offer.

So how do we do our bit to encourage this kind of environment, and how do we create this, at the very least for our own interactions? It is possible, and yet it will likely take some shifts from an old fight-or-flight position to a new mutual respect and connection position. Read on to delve into how to achieve this.

YOUR PREPARATION FOR THE MEETING

Whatever the anticipated atmosphere of your meeting, preparation is crucial. Start by making some notes for what you would like to add to the scheduled meeting. Have these notes in the form of bullet points that you wish to say. That way you can glance at your paper and grab the bullet, then deliver it with eye contact to the group. It will also keep you succinct.

Prepare for any challenges that might come up from the room. What will the doubters say? Write this out and then write out your response. For example, if they are likely to ask 'How can we afford this?' you will need to have a plan in mind to respond.

If you do have a more detailed point to make, advance preparation is even more important. The time it takes will be well rewarded as you will come across as prepared and polished, and you will hold people's attention

- Hook people's attention by defining the problem that you are solving.
- Explain in clear, focused points how the idea solves that problem.
- Describe the actions you need to take.
- Finish up with your proposed action moving forward.

Whatever your desired outcome, if you can turn this into specific, measurable, time orientated actions, with a clarity on what constitutes results, then you'll have clear measurables to work with. This, as you may well know, is called a SMART goal, and is a very useful device for meetings. Write these down, agree them with whoever is involved and then you can follow up by email or in the next meeting. When you have finished your structure, if appropriate, thank people for their attention and ask for input or questions; opening it up to the floor will help open the meeting up again seamlessly.

Top tip: The clearer you can make your request from your team, the more likely it will be achieved. So it's worthwhile getting very clear on your desired outcome prior to the meeting so you can articulate this well.

Set your SMART goals

Here are two useful devices for meetings. SMART goals are very useful for setting your goals and targets. LION is a specific meeting tool to record intentions and keep you focused!

SMART goals are: Specific Measurable Attainable Realistic Timely

A specific goal has a much greater chance of being accomplished than a general goal. To set a specific goal you must answer the six 'W' questions:

Who: Who is involved?

What: What do I want to accomplish?

Where: Identify a location.

When: Establish a time frame.

Which: Identify requirements and constraints.

Why: Specific reasons, purpose or benefits of accomplishing the goal.

EXAMPLE: A general goal would be, 'Get in shape.' But a specific goal would say, 'Join a health club and workout three days a week.

http://topachievement.com/smart.html

LION is a very useful device for structuring a team meeting: Last Issues Opportunities Next

Last week's actions: What did you agree to do last week and have you done it?

Issues: Anything identified from this week's key performance indicators (KPIs); observations by me or her to be discussed. Key result – Get buy-in from both of us on conclusion.

Opportunities: KPIs will show us about an opportunity – i.e. more leads coming in – so anything that needs to be discussed. Get an action from it that we both buy into.

Next week's actions: Record.

How To Listen Well In Meetings

In a meeting, the first essential is to practise active listening as you learnt in Chapter 9. You will find it builds up receptivity, as well as building connections with the other people in the room. I recommend listening as you would like to be listened to: with focused attention, warmth and openness. This means nodding, an open and non-judgemental face and an awareness that it takes courage to share your ideas in public.

THE THREE LEVELS OF LISTENING IN MEETINGS

Listening on level one in a meeting is listening for a moment when you can step in and say your idea. You will need to do some of this, but you certainly don't want to hang out here all the time. Make sure you spend some time in the meeting listening on level two, for the meaning in the words of the people around you, so you are really engaging with their ideas. Then be conscious of level-three listening, where you sit back and listen underneath the words. From this zone you will probably pick up on all sorts of interesting dynamics. You will notice the person who is dying to speak but can't find a way to be heard. You will notice the person who is in an ego place, wanting to take over the room with their energy. You will be able to tune in to them; are they genuine or bluster? You will notice the person who is also calm, biding their time. Perhaps that's you?

Through taking a moment to notice this, it might make you able to support other people in the meeting, directing some of your ideas not to the loudest person but to the person who appears to have something to say. Having listening levels two and three in your meeting tool box will prove invaluable.

BEING GENEROUS IN MEETINGS

Don't be a selfish meeting goer. Because then you have to shout to be heard and you can easily end up in attack-and-defend territory, which, apart from being tiresome, is not very effective. Instead, know that everyone has their own agenda in the meeting and is operating on a personal set of values and standards. Most, if not all, the ideas proposed in the room will have some ego attached, that's just how we operate, so try not to be too judgemental about this. The more you can gently handle other egos whilst putting forward your own ideas, the more receptive they will be to your ideas and the more they will help you to be heard.

CHECK IN AND CHECK OUT

To help with productivity in a meeting, and to ensure a climate of listening, you could do well by having a quick check-in or check-out process.

Check in: If you are chairing the meeting, simply go round at the beginning asking for key goals from the meeting from each person, and possibly anything else they might like to share. This ensures that everyone gets heard and any ideas bursting to get out will be brought to group attention at this point.

Check out: A check-out can be a few questions that each person is asked. This can be a really solid and collaborative way to close a meeting. For example:

- What is one achievement from this meeting you are satisfied with?
- What is one bit of feedback, constructively given, that you may like to offer to improve for next time?
- What is one thing you are proud of from today (or this week)?
- What is one acknowledgement you would like to give someone here?

How To Speak In Meetings

It's important to make the right impression when you do speak – and when you don't. Everyone's eyes will be on you, and they will read the whole of you in order to decide whether to stop and listen, so your non-verbal communication must be as strong as what you actually say.

YOUR NON-VERBAL COMMUNICATION

Sit up straight

This does a few things. It sends signals to your body and brain that you are alert and ready to go, so you will feel more prepared and energised. It allows your voice access to your diaphragm, which means it will come out more powerful and grounded. It looks like you respect yourself and are confident.

Smile

The power of a smile is huge (as seen in Chapter 8), so use it where possible. Of course, it does need to be genuine; if it doesn't feel genuine, avoid it, but try and let your eyes be warm and receptive. Remember the purpose of a smile is to build connection and warmth with others, which should also be in line with your desired outcomes for the meeting.

Gesture and space

Physically taking your space is important. So ensure you are centred in your chair. Use your hands to outline and further emphasise your points. Make sure your shoulders are back. Send the energy outwards rather than inwards, and make eye contact and nod. Own your space and the space around you and, from that place, let your ideas be heard.

Speaking off the cuff

Many people feel fine speaking in meetings if they have prepared, and yet it is the moments where they need to speak off the cuff which they find really challenging. If this is you, then here are some simple guidelines to help you do this.

Step one: If you can, jot down a few points before you speak so you have some sense of what you need to cover. A useful way to quickly structure this is to jot down around five words that represent your points, and then quickly number them in the order you want to deliver. This can take less than a minute to do, and yet will give you total support if your mind goes blank whilst speaking.

Step two: When you are speaking, remember to take pauses and to deliver your ideas to the people in the room with eye contact and intention. By talking steadily (not rushing to get your idea out and your moment over with), you will be able to think as you go, and you will find your thoughts will line up in a far more ordered fashion, waiting for their turn to be spoken.

Step three: Finally, don't allow yourself to get rushed by other people. Find a steady pace and speak clearly. Don't get bullied into inadequate phrasing. Find the right words and give yourself the time you need to do that.

Tip: The important thing to remember is that it doesn't need to be in perfect polished prose. It's not about getting every word right, as people know you haven't prepared, so we judge it with a different criteria than we would if it were a presentation. The important things are: do you give yourself enough time to find the best words? Do you engage with your listeners and paint a picture in their heads? Do you seem enthusiastic about what you are saying? If the answer is yes to these, you are off and away.

Off the cuff exercise...

Pick a subject – anything from a really random subject (such as breakfast) to outlining an article you have just read.

Time yourself for one minute talking on this subject and record yourself speaking.

Write out bullet points of what you have just said.

Now record yourself again, this time being aware of using the key words in each bullet point and using pauses and psychological hooks to pace yourself and keep the interest up (see Chapter 3). You can also use the spoon exercise or the flourish to help you deliver and keep steady (see Chapter 4).

Alternatively, after recording yourself the first time, **listen back**, and **repeat the sentences out loud** (pausing after each sentence), inserting pauses, hooks and using the vowels of important words to ground you and draw attention to them.

⌡ Then try the whole recording again.

⌡ Thirdly, you could **write out the bullet points** (not necessarily in order) and then **record yourself** speaking for one minute, really trying to steadily deliver your ideas.

RESPONDING TO DIFFICULT QUESTIONS

You're asked a question in a meeting and you can't answer it. All eyes are on you, and the thing is… you're not sure what you should say. What to do?

When you don't know the answer

If you can't tell them the answer, then the best thing to do is to be honest and direct. If appropriate, acknowledge the question first, either saying it's a good question or that you understand it and why it has been asked. Then respond honestly. If you don't know the answer, tell them, or ask for time to work it out. If you can partially answer it, do that, then tell them what you would do to find the answer.

Sample deferring lines

- I totally understand why you have asked that question, and I would in your position. However, I don't have the answer to it now as I have been focusing else-where. Can you give me x time (be specific) and I'll let you know.

- That's a great question. The truth is I don't know the answer and I'd rather not give you an estimate. I'd much rather go and find out and get back on (be specific) to you if that's okay.

- That's a great question, and I am so glad you brought it up. It's one I will need to look into further before being ready to answer it.

- I don't know, to be honest with you, but if you give me 24 hours, I will find out and get back to you. Does that work for you?

When you cannot tell them the answer

Or let's say you do know the answer, but it's not your information to give. Here it's about what you say and – surprise, surprise – how you say it. Your delivery needs to be firm and final: a statement. You need to go down at the end in tone, like a powerful full stop. This will clearly mean that the subject is closed.

If you are straight and direct, the questioner will have no way to go with it. They can ask you why you are not prepared, but essentially, once they hit your integrity, there is nowhere to go from there.

If people question why, tell them the truth as far as you are able. If you state the truth, your truth, with a clear definitive tone, then there is no budge from there. No one can force you to say what you don't want to say, so being honest about this is the most powerful response you can have. Be prepared for the frustration of others, and to simply and respectfully hold your ground.

Sample deferring lines

*   I don't feel comfortable discussing that, I'm afraid.

*   While I appreciate why you want to know, I am not prepared to answer that at this time.

What you want to avoid is getting flustered or making excuses, or trying to fake it or hide it. If you do that, a certain kind of person will smell blood and go after you till they make you squirm. A brutal and very obvious example of this is the interviewer, Jeremy Paxman.

Below is a script of a challenging interview between Jeremy Paxman and a young minister, Chloe Smith. In it he is drilling her for an answer which she is avoiding. Rather than simply state her position, she tries to play his game, and the more she avoids it, the more he goes in for the kill. It's like watching a slaughter. I have put a rewrite below in line with our four key steps, so we can see an alternative.

Case study: A lamb to the slaughter

CS: This has been under consideration for some time.

JP: When was the decision taken?

CS: As I say, this has been under consideration for some time, the Chancellor and the Prime Minister take the decision between them.

JP: So when were you told then?

CS: I've been involved for some time and the ...

Previously, it's possible she could have just misunderstood his need to know exact dates and times, but now he has repeated it, she would

*have fared better if she'd answered his question directly at this point.
She could have said: 'I'm not able to give you the exact time I was
told.' To which, terrier-like Paxman would say, 'Why not?' to which she
could simply respond, 'It's not appropriate and I'm not prepared to.'
But she didn't do that. Read on to see the painful mauling that follows.*

JP: But you didn't take the decision, obviously; the
Chancellor and Prime Minister did – yes? So when you
were told?

CS: We had a collective discussion of that er...er in
due course and although I can't, you know, give you the
sort of gory details of all the processes.

*Chloe is trying to keep her cool, but has made the mistake of trying to
belittle his need to know by using the phrase 'gory details' instead of
respecting why he wants to know, and respecting her inability to say.*

JP: Well, did it happen today?

CS: I can't, I can't, I can't sit here and tell you
the ins and the outs.

JP: You can't remember.

CS: No, it's not appropriate for me to tell you
the ins and outs.

This is good – much more direct.

JP: Why isn't it appropriate? You are coming
here to defend a change of policy and you
can't even tell me when you were told what
the change in policy was.

CS: Because as a minister in the treasury I have
been involved in discussions for some time,
as I've said to you, the Chancellor and the
Prime Minister take those decisions.

*Clear and direct – this is much better. She was delivering
these lines with firmness and clarity too.*

JP: Right.

CS: I'm not going to be able to give you a
running commentary .

This moment is very interesting. Chloe had just found her feet, and she had quietened Jeremy Paxman. When she firmly said, 'I'm not going to be able', she could have closed the discussion by saying 'to give you any more information than that. I understand you want to know, but it's not appropriate that I go into detail on exact dates and times.'

By using the phrase 'running commentary' she was patronising his need to know instead of understanding it and respecting it. And he didn't like it. So he went in for the kill again.

> **JP** (back in the game): I'm not asking for a running commentary. I'm asking for a statement of facts about when you were told. You were told sometime today, clearly. Was it before lunch or after lunch?

> **CS:** I'm not going to give you... a commentary on who says what and when.

Oh dear – referred again to running commentary – so she is back in hot water!

> **JP:** NO, I just want to know when you were told. I'm not even going to ask you who told you but when were you told what the policy was?

> **CS:** This has been under discussion for some weeks.

> **JP:** Right, and at some point during those several weeks, they communicated to you there had been a decision to change policy.

At this point he let her off this hook – he had other ones to catch her with next. [7]

Overall, it was an embarrassing display which could have been avoided if she had acknowledged his position and clearly shared her own. Instead of which, she chose to patronise him, which only spurred him on to go for her even more. She was like the mouse to Paxman's cat.

There are two morals to this story:

- Don't step in to the battlefield unless you're really sure you want a fight and you're really sure you can win.

- Be direct. Honesty is powerful.

Interrupting Well

It's come to the point where you want to step in, but the voices are so loud, how will you do it and be heard? Well, there is a super-simple, incredibly usable foolproof little device you can use to achieve this.

INTERRUPT WITH SOMETHING NICE

Beginning with something nice will make the loudest person in the room be quiet to listen to you. If you start a sentence with a negative, chances are they won't want to hear it. And for those who can, they might well talk over you. How many times have you heard someone interrupt with 'the problem with that is...' or 'no...' or 'but...'? None of these is a good interjection. Would you want to stop talking?

However, start a sentence with 'great...' or 'yes..' or 'that's a great idea...' and you have instant receptivity and a warm feeling.

This isn't just a trick. It is about respecting the process of communication, which is an exchange of ideas, thoughts and feelings between at least two people. It's polite and respectful to receive a person's idea before offering your own. The idea of an interjection that simply interrupts with your own idea is ultimately a selfish one. Yes, you may have something you want to say, but you also need to give them something they want to hear. I have put a couple of examples below.

Sample interruptions

* That's a great idea. What I really like about that is...

* That's an interesting approach, and I think a lot of benefit could be found in it.

Another idea to add to the mix…

Top tip: Please don't follow the positive statement with a 'but'. It's important to find the positive in what is being said in order to make people receptive to your idea. It can't be a trick (because then it will only work once) so you need to genuinely find positive things to say. At the very least, it could be an interesting approach.

FOUR STEPS TO BEING INTERRUPTED WELL

Ever been interrupted in a meeting? Probably. Ever been in the middle or at the beginning of an interesting point and have someone step in and talk right over you as if they didn't even notice you were speaking? Likely.

Interrupting happens all the time. As you know from above, there is a right and a wrong way to do it. So what to do if it happens to you?

First, try not to obey any angry amygdala reflexes that make you want to yell or weep (the amygdala is the part of your brain – some call it the lizard brain – that houses the fight-or-flight reflexes). Secondly, either decide to let it go and pick up your point later, or you might want to do something about it. Thirdly, if any negative voices come in to your head – either about you like 'I'm just boring' or about them 'they are so intolerable' – bat them away. They are not helpful here. Everyone has a right to a voice; remember the principle of commitment?

Now, let's say you've had enough of being interrupted and you want to take action. Remember, we all have the right to the same air. And you deserve to speak if you have something to say. So here's how.

Step one

Firstly, you can stop them in their tracks by saying as loudly as you need to be heard, 'Excuse me.' This is best low and firm but clearly audible. You might have some adrenalin left over from the amygdala flare-up, so you can use it here (although make sure you remain calm).

Step two

Now you have got their attention, hold it with intention for a moment. This is crucial. This is when you take back ownership of the space, claiming your right to speak. Remember the power of the pause. This is it right here. You are bringing the energy back to you, bringing the attention back to you, and also, crucially, calming down.

Step three

Now, calmly and with your grounded voice, start speaking – any of the examples below would be fine, or one of your own. The main thing is to ensure you don't say it with anger. Just clearly, politely and firmly.

- I hadn't quite finished.
- I was just making a point and I hadn't finished; would you mind letting me finish and then I'd really like to hear your point.
- I'd really like to finish my point, if that's okay with you.
- You just interrupted me. Would you mind if I finish?

If they say, 'I had a point I just wanted to make,' you decide whether to hold the floor or not. The likelihood is they will apologise and politely (and maybe slightly awkwardly or embarrassed) say, 'Sure'.

Step four

Be gracious – when you have finished your point, you can direct it at them, smile, or say thank you. Reward them for giving you space. That way you are positively reinforcing their good behaviour, making it more likely they will let you speak next time. Avoid making them feel chagrined or smaller for interrupting you. Although it may be tempting to ignore them as you speak, particularly if all eyes are on you, and it feels like you've been successful in taking back the talking stick, please don't. Punishment (in this case embarrassing them) is proven to be far, far less productive in terms of leading to desired outcomes.

LSW Gem: I'm not playing ball

An interesting way to look at it is as if the interruption were a ball. They have thrown a ball at you when they interrupted. With your 'excuse me' you catch the ball, take it over to your side. Then the pause is where you hold the ball and put it calmly on the table. You are not playing ball but having an adult conversation. The important moment here, the transformative moment, is actually not when you grab the ball, but when you place the ball on the table. You have everyone's attention, you have the ball, and everyone thinks you will throw it. But you don't. You place the ball on the table and, in that pause, you find your grounded voice, from which you can make one of the statements above.

Case study: A successful interruption

The meeting is in full throttle, voices are being raised, and ideas bandied about. This does make you feel a little shy, but you have done your preparation and know you can do this. You have a particular idea you want to share that you think will really add to the mix. You don't want to shout or compete for space. You have your notes in front of you which outline the idea and respond to possible challenges. You couldn't be more prepared if you tried. The moment is here. You sit up straight in your seat, breathe deeply and interject in a clear, low voice. Everyone turns to listen to you. You smile and make eye contact with the people at the table.

You explain you have an idea and request their attention. They give it willingly. When you have finished two minutes later, there is a buzz of questions. You answer them steadily, never flustered, and then you get your first nod of approval.

'I like it,' your manager says. 'I want to see a more detailed brief on my desk by the end of this week with a strategy for *getting it off the ground in three months' time,'* he says. This is great, but not perfect, and you were prepared for this.

'*I'd like to give it the attention required but have most of my time taken up with the current project. I have looked into what's necessary and can do it in four days if I can have Cathy full time to balance the load.*' 'Agreed,' your manager says, amused. You've done it.

How to be efficient and productive in meetings
/ GOLDEN RULES /

1. Know your core beliefs for the meeting and stand by them.

2. Use all your listening skills.

3. Always interject with something nice to create a receptive atmosphere and show respect.

4. If someone interrupts you, stop them, take a moment to neutralise the energy, and then carry on calmly and without tension.

5. Make sure your body language helps you out – good posture and use of hands to send confident signals to your brain.

6. Prepare your points, and plan for difficult questions and actions you want to be carried out. It is much more likely to happen.

Chapter 12 | How to be angry with grace |

In this chapter you will learn about:

- **Big ideas for peaceful communication:** Establishing the principles
- **Non-violent communication:** And the notions of winners and losers
- **How to succeed at difficult conversations:** Six practical steps.

While we may approach a difficult conversation thinking we have it all mapped out, we have all experienced those occasions where it spirals out of control. This can leave us feeling more than a little confused or regretful and yet, if you have some powerful tools at your disposal, you can almost always keep your anger in check and avoid the difficult consequences of losing your temper.

THIS CHAPTER OFFERS A SET OF THEORETICAL TOOLS around how to handle difficult conversations generally, provides a framework to support that and gives practical steps on what to do. A lot of the ideas are based on a practice called non-violent communication, a game-changing methodology which has been used successfully to reduce conflict around the world. I took a nine-week course in NVC in San Francisco a few years ago, and have distilled it into the method here. If you are intrigued to find out more, please read Marshall Rosenberg's *Non-violent Communication*.

A difficult scenario

You run a small firm of architects with a handful of small and medium-sized clients and three architects who work for you. Three months ago you took on Katie, a receptionist who doubles up as office manager and administrator. She was great in the interview but in the last month she has become increasingly more sullen and surly.

She never smiles at clients and the waiting area has become somewhere people hate to hang about in. You decide you must speak to her, and really you just want her to leave. You book a time with her and find yourself feeling nervous. She is actually a little scary, you realise – all frowns and scowls. You decide to take the tough approach, and that you won't take any rudeness from her or she is out. The scene goes like this.

You: Hi Katie, come in, take a seat. (Katie sits down.)

So I've asked you in today because, quite frankly, I'm just not happy with how you have been with our clients.

Katie: What do you mean?

You: They find you rude and sullen. You are monosyllabic with them, and at worst rude, at best just unpleasant. It's really not tolerable. (Katie's jaw clenches.)

Katie: Right.

(You had expected something different. Now what?)

You: Well, do you have anything to say?

Katie: If you feel like that, then fine. I'm not sure there is anything I can say. You've told me they find me unpleasant. I find them rude. And other people in the office rude. So forgive me if I don't come in all smiles.

You: Well Katie, you are the receptionist. It's your job to smile and make people welcome.

Katie: Oh really. Is that my job? Because I thought my job was answering phones and sending emails and letters and organising three architects' diaries. Oh and managing the office and ordering in stationery. And organising meetings and booking plane and train tickets, conferences and events, confirming meetings, and running the customer management system. Have I missed anything? Hmmm. I'm not sure.

You: Oh.

Katie: I'm sick of feeling under-appreciated and overworked. You know what? This is the most horrible

> job I've ever had. I'm sorry but I've had enough. I
> quit. That's me done.
>
> Katie walks out the room leaving you stunned.
> Hmmm. That didn't go as planned. Now not only do
> you feel terrible, you have to find a receptionist at
> the last minute. Plus you realise in less than a day
> just how capable Katie was.

Big Ideas For Peaceful Communication

This section will begin with some powerful ideas that will help you deal
with those difficult conversations.

DON'T WRITE SOMEONE'S SCRIPT FOR THEM

Have you ever thought someone was annoyed with you, come up with ideas
on why they were annoyed, and then got mad at them because you feel what
you think they are thinking is unfair? Most of us do similar silly things; it's
human nature. However, even though you often think you know what is
going on in someone's head, with a certainty you would be willing to bet
money on, don't assume that you are right. Sometimes we are right, but
often we are not.

Nobel prize winner Daniel Kahneman's award-winning book, *Thinking, Fast
and Slow,* explored this idea, that we often have an intuitive sense that we
believe to be right, but actually this feeling that we know what is going on is
just that, a feeling. So don't jump to conclusions about what is going on for
someone else, ask them. This alone will avoid all manner of difficult situations with people.

WHAT WE THINK ABOUT WE MAKE MANIFEST

If you think enough about something, you will to some degree manifest it in
your experience. This idea can be seen on many different levels and is very
powerful. On a simple level, if you think long and hard about a red Porsche,
you will likely start to see lots of them everywhere. You are not creating red
Porsches, but you are telling your unconscious mind to notice them where
you wouldn't have noticed them before. Similarly, if you think you attract
difficult people, and as such have arguments a lot, then guess what? You'll
find lots of difficult people around you, who you argue with. If we have an
interpretation of the world, and then we interpret the world to support that,
pretty soon, our world can become that (for us). What we believe becomes

a self-fulfilling prophecy. So be wary of your thoughts. This is particularly relevant around difficult conversations because the ideas and stories we enter the conversation with, can all too easily be played out if we don't consciously change them. So if you go into a difficult conversation thinking that person B is very tricky and you must prepare for a fight, then chances are your behaviour will encourage her to let out her tricky side, and you'll be reinforcing your belief.

The good news is you can change this, first by noticing that you have a choice in your thoughts about person B, and then thinking new thoughts about person B.

WHAT FIRES TOGETHER WIRES TOGETHER

In short, we can change the way we think. If we have a behavioural pattern – let's say we get into arguments easily and are considered argumentative or even aggressive – then this is not a temperament we are stuck with. In the last ten years, huge discoveries have been made around what's called the neuroplasticity of the brain. Rather than the brain being developmentally fixed past a certain age, which is what they used to believe, they discovered the brain is never fixed. There is always the potential for brain development. This can be as simple as learning new skills, or as complex as training a part of your brain to literally change its functionality. What this means for us is that what we think and our behaviours and patterns of behaviour become hardwired into our brains. If, for example, you find you are always getting into arguments and you want to do something about it, you could take on the methodology in this chapter, practise repeatedly and, after a time, the new patterns would become second nature, a part of your brain. What fires together wires together.

THE ANGRY AMYGDALA

When our brain developed, one of the early parts of it was the amygdala. We share this part with all mammals, and it houses, among other things, our fight-or-flight reflex. As our brains developed, we grew the cerebral cortex, which essentially houses our ability to make rational judgements, to think things through. One way of thinking about this is to return to the concept of our chimp brain and our adult brain.

If we act according to our amygdala, or base impulses, we have little control over our responses, and this can lead to a dangerous spiral of anger being met with more anger. If, however, we wait a moment, our higher-functioning cerebral cortex kicks in. This is where we can make reasonable, rational value judgements about what to do. So have you ever heard about counting to five if you are angry? Well, there is good reason for this. By the time you reach five, your cerebral cortex is back in the driving seat, dealing with the information and working out the best approach.

So if something riles you, don't let yourself be guided by your limbic brain. Wait, breathe for a few seconds, then shift from the unconscious response to your cerebral cortex and make rational decisions on how to handle it.

PEOPLE WANT TO FEEL RECOGNISED

If you want to resolve something peacefully, there is a really simple way to achieve it. Make someone feel heard, understood, acknowledged. If you take time to try to understand their position, even if you don't agree with it, you are creating a fertile soil for change and negotiation to take place. If you can show that you recognise their values and needs, if you can acknowledge something positive, then this takes them out of the space of defensive or offensive and into a space of openness.

Why? Well, people are not going to disagree with you if you give them genuine recognition. If you can start here, in any difficult conversation, then you are starting at a place of peace.

Non-Violent Communication

A difficult conversation that goes wrong can lead to a cacophony of negative emotions. And there are only ever a few outcomes:

- Everyone is angry.

- There is a winner and a loser.

- The loser feels either like a victim, unfairly mistreated, leaving them bitter and resentful, or angry and biding their time.

- The winner may feel powerful, but this kind of power is unhealthy. It is the power of warfare, and one battle follows another unless peace is created.

This method is about stopping warfare, stopping attacks or counter-attacks, stopping power struggles, victims and vanquishers. You have to be convinced that all of the above are not useful for you to take on this method. It is new, and involves a shift.

Dealing with conflict is not about winning, but about peace and mutual respect. At the heart are some core ideas. If you want to learn how to win a conflict, this is not the place. This way is different and is based on the simple ideas described above. It was developed by Marshall Rosenberg in the 1940s.

TENET ONE: THERE IS NO RIGHT AND WRONG

If we want to arrive at a peaceful resolution we have to let go of right and wrong.

In most arguments, we tend to go in with the idea that we are right and other people wrong. Or that there is a right and wrong and the purpose of the argument is to find out which is which, get everyone to agree and move forward. It's a very human position to take. However, it is totally unhelpful, and this is why.

There is very little to be achieved through the right/wrong concept. If I make myself right and you wrong, then we are just caught in the web of defensiveness, blame, power and attack. NVC points out that even if you come out a winner in the old right/wrong paradigm, you leave with a thin triumph of ego rather than a healthy communication transaction.

No one wants to be wrong, so they either submit with lots of negative emotions or fight and try and make themselves right.

Out beyond ideas of wrongdoing and right-doing, there is a field. I'll meet you there.

Rumi

In this beautiful Rumi line, he understands that blame and accusation are useless if one wants to 'meet' another person. And 'meeting' really is the point of good communication. All you have with right and wrong are a winner and a loser, or continued war. Therefore, if we want to come to a place of peace with someone, we need to let go of right and wrong.

Even if only one person refuses to go there, you still come closer to peace because in order to have a winner or loser it takes two people to engage in the right/wrong idea. If you have one person refusing to go there, then it's not possible. The results are incredible.

TENET TWO: ALL ACTIONS ARE STRATEGIES AROUND MET OR UNMET VALUES AND NEEDS

All actions are based on trying to get our values met. All values are clean. So, if we let go of right and wrong, what is there? Well, the answer is simple and it starts with understanding.

NVC states that at the core of all actions are human values and needs, like love, respect, achievement, connection. All values and needs are equal and all are neutral and clean. It also states that every single action we take is the result of our values and needs either being met or not met. Again, there are no right and wrong actions, instead there are effective and ineffective strategies.

This means if we can try to understand the values underlining the other person's actions, then we can speak to them with empathy, even if we disagree with their actions. John Assaraf, motivational speaker, author and philanthropist, says that most arguments emerge simply from a difference in values. If I value family and you value creativity, you will find it difficult when I nag you to spend time with the kids when you are in the middle of a painting, and I will find it difficult to accept that you would rather paint than spend time with the kids. If one can respect that different values dominate for different people, it's a great start to good communication. It doesn't mean the outcome is always going to be easy to find, but it does mean there is a basis of respect, which is essential to a good outcome. This understanding helps remove the anger and replace it with empathy, which means that you won't enter into the conversation in attack mode, and they therefore won't step into that game and either attack back or become defensive.

TENET THREE: THERE ARE NO WRONG ACTIONS, JUST INEFFECTIVE STRATEGIES

So if someone does something that seems outwardly really bad, then rather than label this as bad, we can look to see the value leading to the ineffective strategy. For example, a gang member is desperate to belong. To feel he is not alone, he does terrible things to be part of the gang. The terrible things do not make him wrong, they are his strategies to meet his need, which is to be loved or to belong. The strategies may be ineffective in that he ends up in prison, feeling even more unloved, but he is not wrong.

This idea helps us to gain empathy and understanding for other people's actions, even really horrible ones, because it helps us to see the human beneath the action. This allows for a basis for communication no matter who does what.

TENET FOUR: THE WAY TO PEACE IS TO BE AN ADVOCATE OF OUR OWN AND THE OTHER PERSON'S VALUES

This final tenet is very beautiful. It asks us to find out the values motivating the other person's behaviour, and then be an advocate of both their values and our own. It asks for mutual respect of every being, and paves the way for forgiveness and for peaceful resolution. It's incredibly powerful because it takes away any space for accusation and the usual (and mostly unsuccessful) rounds of defence and attack.

So if you like the sound of this, read on.

How To Succeed At Difficult Conversations

What do you do when you have something difficult to say to someone? Blurt it right out? Build yourself into a state of vexation until you are so angry with them you don't care how they react? Attempt a half measure and come out of the conversation furious at yourself for not saying what you needed to say?

We all find those difficult conversations a challenge to varying degrees. Many people dislike confrontation so much that they will do anything to avoid it, even stepping out of the situation entirely rather than confronting it. In this section, we offer you another way, a way to lead a difficult conversation that doesn't result in anger on your part or defensiveness on theirs.

There are six steps. The first two are essential. Steps three and four can be done in any order.

STEP ONE: ATTITUDE SHIFT

Be an advocate of their needs as well as your own.

Something has happened and you are angry. You don't like how an employee has behaved, how a friend has treated you, something a colleague has done. It's time to have a difficult conversation.

The first thing you need to do is shift your attitude. It needs to move away from right and wrong, to one of recognising everyone is simply doing their best to meet their own needs. Not one of blame and status, but one of seeking to find a positive solution for everyone.

This means feeling your anger, but being prepared to also build an understanding of what is going on for the other person. To be an advocate of your own needs, you need to understand what has annoyed you. Then to be an advocate of theirs, you need to try to think about why they are behaving the way they are, and what values underlie their behaviour.

Ask yourself: Why am I really annoyed here? What values are not being met?

Ask yourself: What might be going on for them? What values or needs are they honouring by behaving the way they are behaving? What, if any, values and needs might not be getting met?

STEP TWO: RECOGNITION AND ACKNOWLEDGEMENT

If we see the good in people we very often get it.

People thrive on praise and wither on criticism. If you begin a difficult conversation with someone by recognising what they are doing well, you create receptivity for whatever you are about to say.

Our expectations of the individual, positive or negative, are far more likely to become the reality. If we see the good in people, they are likely to behave in that way. So if we treat someone and communicate with someone as if they are full of potential, if we appeal to the best in someone, then they can far more easily conform to that, and vice versa. If we call someone a bad person and a tyrant, then it's more likely they will act that way. A look at our criminal justice system confirms this. With an attitude that people are guilty and should be punished, we lock them up, and the reoffending rate is around 70%. In Norway, where they treat prisoners not so much like deviants but like people who can improve and make good decisions, they have a 16% reoffending rate.

So if you need to give someone an official warning, tell them their work isn't good enough, or air a grievance on a personal level, if you can find a way to say something that recognises them or their position before you share yours, it's very powerful.

Ask yourself: What are their values? Where are they doing really well? Where are they resonating with this work?

Case study: Positivity in action

Some time ago I had the privilege of seeing this in action with someone who works for me. I was unhappy with their attitude, and it had been brewing for weeks, to the point that I had the feeling it wasn't going to work and was planning to give them an official warning. I didn't like their communication, and being a company that teaches it, I was very unhappy to have a member of staff who was underperforming in this area.

However, I knew also that it was worthwhile doing what I could to get the best out of this person, and knowing these techniques, I planned how I would approach it.

I told this person I respected them and their ability, and yet there were certain things that just weren't good enough. I invited them to step up, and also stated that this might not be the right job for them and if so I would fully respect them anyway.

What happened over the next days and weeks was pretty remarkable. The individual did a total about turn. Their attitude shifted, all of their communication went from difficult to delightful, and they became a pleasure to work with. When I spoke to them a few weeks later, full of praise about the shift, they told me what had made the real difference was the fact I had said that I respected their talent and ability. Even though I knew this, it still amazed me that, out of all the words I had said, the ones that they most needed to hear were recognition. But there it is. This stuff works. If we see the best in people, we very often get it.

STEP THREE: LISTENING TO THE OTHER PERSON

Knowing where the other person is at, and what is going on for them, puts you in a far more informed position.

The order of this step and the next depends largely on the dynamic of the relationship and the situation, and can be changed to what feels most instinctive and appropriate. It can sometimes be easier if you hear the other person first, so that you can build that understanding into what you say. However, sometimes you might simply need to speak, and if that is the case, you must follow that instinct. Whatever the order, make sure that you have created a safe space for them to share how they are feeling constructively.

Ask open questions, find out what is going on for them. If you think you know which values they are adhering to, ask them if that is the case. If you don't know what values are driving their actions, then ask questions to find out. It might be that your values are so different that you can't find a middle ground. But at least you can part company with mutual respect. Because remember, all values are equal.

With this step, the other person could get aggressive, depending on if and for how long they have been harbouring ill feelings. If this happens it's important to manage it with calm to prevent it from going badly. Again, it can be as simple as acknowledging that you've heard them and their position.

You can use neutral lines like:

* *It sounds like you are pretty frustrated.*
* *It sounds like that was pretty tough for you.*
* *I can hear that you haven't been happy.*
* *It seems like you are a bit upset right now.*

Language tip: It's important you don't put words in their mouth. Using the phrase 'it sounds like' is a pretty safe bet. Ask them how they feel things are going. What do they want to share?

STEP FOUR: SHARING YOUR POSITION

When you are sharing your position, it's important that you simply share the facts that led to your feelings. Prior to the discussion, get really clear on what the issue is, which values aren't being met (if you haven't done this in step one) and which of their actions or lack of actions caused the issue for you. List out the facts of it. There should be no judgement or evaluation or subjective terms creeping in.

Here are some examples of judgemental and factual comments:

Judgemental comments	Factual comments
You've been ridiculously late nine times out of ten!	In the last month there have been 13 instances when you have been between 20 and 40 minutes late.
That was so stupid of you to build a wall 20cm higher than I'd asked! You never listen to me!	You clearly aren't bothered about this job. You are rude to clients and you continually make mistakes.
You clearly aren't bothered about this job. You are rude to clients and you continually make mistakes.	In the last week I have received two complaints from clients who felt unhappy about how you spoke to them. There have also been three mistakes in the last week.

This is crucial because it takes the emotion out of the situation and just offers up a clean objectivity. It's difficult to do, though – and as soon as you bring subjective terms in, the other person can start to react – so really try and watch yourself here!

Ask yourself: what are the actual facts and events that led to the problem? What is an objective and neutral description of the situation?

STEP FIVE : SHARING YOUR VALUES AND NEEDS

Next you can explain what your feelings are about this, and which needs or values aren't or weren't being met. To find your unmet needs and values, go deeper into your feelings and ask yourself why you feel this way. If you are honest with yourself you'll soon get to what is underneath. And remember as you do this not to make the other person wrong, that it is all relative. This means you take responsibility for your feelings and your needs by separating your feelings from your needs and taking the time to understand what is actually going on for you, beneath the top-line emotion.

This is really helpful to avoid judgement and accusation. And by simply expressing your feelings, there is an element of honesty and responsibility here, very different from what we might usually do in an angry situation (which is usually filled with accusation and blame). By communicating in this way, it takes the heat out of it for the listener and usually helps them to hear you much more clearly.

To continue with our example above, you might say any of the following:

- *I feel frustrated when I have members of staff who come in late, as it appears they don't respect me or the job or company.*

- *As the owner of this company, I can't run things efficiently when members of staff are consistently late.*

- *I value efficiency. As such, lateness is really not acceptable for me.*

LSW Gem: Things to avoid

Any of these will take you back to the war zone pretty quickly!

- Blame.
- Stating anything subjective as fact.
- Accusing with the word 'you' – you did, you are.

Ask yourself: what do you feel? Is it frustrated, upset, annoyed, disappointed? Ask yourself why you feel that, what needs or values have not been met?

STEP SIX: ASK FOR WHAT YOU WOULD LIKE MOVING FORWARD

This is the point where you get to ask for the actions you want that will make it better. It doesn't mean you will get it, but in asking, you can really move things forward. This step is the most productive, in many ways the most simple, but also the most difficult. It is difficult because it makes us feel vulnerable. Because implicit in it is the risk they may say no. It takes courage to state what we really want and leave ourselves open to the other person having the power to grant that or not. It also means we move away from a place of blame and feeling right, or self righteousness, which can feel powerful, to a place that is more open and receptive to finding harmony, compromise and moving forward. And that can be a tough transition to make. However, if we'd rather move forward in our relationships, out of sticky areas of tension and into productive collaboration, then this request is the way to do it. It is incredibly powerful.

- *I request that whatever it is you are dealing with in the morning, you do after work, and you come early.*

- *I will also ask that you come to me with issues rather than turning up late. As you know this is important for me, I need to be very clear that I won't tolerate any more lateness if you haven't discussed it with me, okay?*

- *Is that fair enough?*

Ask yourself: What is it you would like them to do? What are the simple actions they could take that would mean your need or value is met?

LSW Gem: Peaceful communication when you are angry

I not you: Keep statements in first person to take responsibility for your own feelings, rather than pointing an accusatory finger.

Facts not opinion: If you need to explain what they are doing that isn't working for you, keep to the facts. Don't mix it up with your evaluation of the facts.

Open questions: Ask open questions to get at what is behind their behaviour, which might be useful in order to motivate them as an employee, and to make sure they feel important and want to do their best for you.

Empowering questions: You can also use a question to make a request. What are they willing to do to correct the issue? This is a very empowering approach, and rather than giving orders allows the individual to feel you have enough faith in them to get them to come up with the solution.

Empowering people: The more you give people the right kind of instruction that allows them to take ownership of the task, and give them the impetus to do it, the more they will surprise and amaze you at how productive they can be. As long as you keep recognising their work, this can keep on growing.

Avoid rigid instructions: If, on the other hand, you give microscopic instructions on how they should do their job, the individual will feel patronised and become more rigid.

Scenario: Replay the scenario

At the beginning of this chapter, we saw Katie make a hasty exit. But now you've read this book and we can replay the scene. Katie comes in and you say hello.

> **You:** Katie, I've asked you to come in today because I feel like there are some things that aren't quite working, and I suspect that there might be some things for you as well. I want to discuss them openly and honestly and see if we can't find a way to solve it. How does that sound?
>
> **Katie:** Okay.
>
> **You:** I want you to know that I've thought about your work here and realise you have been taking on a lot of additional responsibilities and handling those well and I want to recognise you for that. Well done.
>
> **Katie** (her face beginning to look a little lighter for the first time in months): Thank you.
>
> **You:** As we both know, some aspects of your role have not been working so well. It seems like you are not happy and that is getting picked up by staff and clients too. As front of house, it's important we make the right impression, so this needs to be discussed. I would like to know your thoughts on this, how are you doing? What's going on for you?

At this point Katie opens up. She has felt overworked, stressed and unappreciated.

> **You:** Katie, it sounds like it's been a difficult period for you and I'm sorry to hear that you've felt unsupported. I want to work out some solutions to that with you. On the same note, it's really important that we address this issue of creating the right environment for staff and clients. Reasonable?
>
> **Katie:** I think so.
>
> **You:** Good. It's important that this works both ways. Let's discuss some actions we can take to make you feel more supported, and some actions you can take to make clients feel more welcome when they come in.

The next phase of the conversation is about some concrete agreements that work for everyone. You may agree a trial period for both of you and to reconvene in two weeks.

The shift in the scenario above shows how you can pull a relationship back from the brink and into the realms of two people working to make it function again. If we were to boil it down to one thing – it is about the power of empathy to shift someone from angry and defensive to open and receptive.

What you'll find using these techniques in conversations is that they get cleaner and are resolved much more quickly.

How to be angry with grace
/ GOLDEN RULES /

1. Don't go in with expectations about what is going on for the other person, be prepared to find out.

2. Think about why you're annoyed, which values and needs are not being met.

3. Think about why they might be behaving in the way they are, what values or needs might they be pursuing by their behaviour.

4. Be prepared to find something positive in their behaviour, to let them know you are not criticising them for the sake of it.

5. When you state what has led to your annoyance, make sure that you keep to the objective details and avoid any subjectivity, evaluation or accusation.

6. Be clear on your request to them, and use an empowering question if appropriate to involve them in the solution.

Chapter 13 | How to calm an angry person |

> **In this chapter you will learn about:**
>
> - **Handling someone else's anger:** Five practical steps
> - **Sorry:** How to use the hardest word
> - **Peaceful communication:** Tops tips on how it should be done

This chapter gives you an overview, tips, insights and concrete steps for what to do if someone is angry with you. It's not easy or pleasant being in the firing line, but the steps in this chapter will help you to manage it, whether you are guilty or not. It will also support you to stay calm, avoid some of the cardinal sins, and give you the tools to come out, at best, with a more productive relationship or, at worst, relatively unscathed. They are basically the same techniques we described in the previous chapter, so if you are dipping into the book, I suggest you read Chapter 12 before you start on this one.

SO WE'VE COVERED WHAT TO DO with your own anger, but what if someone is angry with you? The steps, unsurprisingly, are very similar. One of the biggest skills here is listening and not reacting, which can take some practice and a lot of breathing!

A client, friend or colleague calls you up or storms in your office and starts yelling at you. What do you do? You might well have an instant gut reaction which involves defending yourself against their attack or staging a counter-attack.

But both of those will get you firmly into the land of right and wrong, and with that into the battle zone. As we have seen, the battle zone is only good for winning and losing, not for collaboration and peace. On the battleground, the strongest will win. And if you are receiving feedback from your boss, likelihood is it will be him.

So, assuming we are on the same page, let's look at what to do. As before, there are a series of steps with lots of similarities to handling your own anger; however, they have some small adjustments.

Worst-case scenario

The worst has happened. You've been juggling a new job with moving house and a new relationship, and from feeling like you can manage everything, your world has begun to implode. Balls are being dropped, and yesterday, for the second time this month, you forgot to remind your boss of an important meeting you had scheduled in for him. The result: he missed it and is now furious with you. You know you are in trouble.

He calls you into his office and tells you, without mincing his words, that you are at last-chance saloon. As soon as he gives you a chance to speak, you start to explain, excuses bubble up one after the other.

To which he replies he doesn't give a sh** and that you are an adult and if you can't handle a job then you don't deserve to have one.

You try again to tell him it's a one-off and it's the house move, but he walks out saying as he leaves, one more chance.

Couldn't have gone worse, really.

Figure 13.1
Communication Aikido

Handling Someone Else's Anger

STEP ONE: ATTITUDE SHIFT AND RECEIVE

At the very first moment of being attacked, we have a few options: we tense up to receive the attack and get ready to defend ourselves; we charge at the attacker with all our energy, hitting them back with a similar amount of energy to what they came at us with; we do some communication aikido.

One and two are not helpful options. You either get beaten up or enter into a fight, neither of which is good in the long term. So let's look at three.

You might find that you will have an initial fight-or-flight reaction. However, it's important you don't react straight away. If you feel a surge of anger, breathe a little and wait for it to pass. The anger will be coming from the home of your fight-or-flight reflex, the amygdala. When you breathe, try and take a breath deep into your belly (read the chapter on vocal impact if you would like to get more technical about this) and then focus on the exhale. You could try to count to five in your head as you breathe out. And by this time, you are likely to feel back in control.

Once control has been regained, all you need to do at this point is listen. It's crucial that you don't absorb their energy, but you just sit and hear it out until they've got it off their chest. Know that with aikido you take energy and move it away. Your body doesn't need to be tense. In fact, the more relaxed you are, the more effective you are in just releasing their energy. Breathing is useful here. Managing your breath will help to keep you calm.

Even if you think the person accusing you is totally unjustified, try to understand where they are coming from. If you write them off as wrong or unreasonable, then that will usually heighten their anger and their attack. Better to try and get your head round where they are and what has annoyed them. If they value running a successful business, if they value efficiency, or excellence or independence, in what way are their values not being met?

If you feel up to it, you can also take a second step, and just make a gentle ahh sound or anything neutral and relatively meaningless like 'okay' or 'right'. It's the verbal equivalent of the nod, and it's just a sound which says you are listening and taking no stance.

That's it. Aikido communication done.

Now we move onto a new metaphor. Imagine their attack is an apple. You have taken it, taken a look at it, and put it on the table.

STEP TWO: SEEKING UNDERSTANDING AND LISTENING

This is your opportunity to seek further clarification if you don't fully understand their anger. It helps you to show them that you are really engaging with their issue. It also gives them a chance to speak and defuses the situation further. From your point of view, you cannot move towards an apology for something you are not sure about.

You can use lines like the following:

- *It sounds like x is the problem. Is that right?*

- *From what I understand, xx has happened. Is that the case?*

- *Are you saying...?*

- *So you feel that...?*

- *Just to get clear. Is the thing that is making you unhappy x?*

- *It sounds like you have been pretty frustrated. Can you tell me more?*

Now you wait while they respond. They may be rude and aggressive again or they may calm themselves down. If they are rude, depending on the situation, you may choose to calmly deal with this. If, for example, you are on a customer service team and not directly responsible for their attack, it might feel appropriate to say something, before moving on. If, on the other hand, they are your boss, then it might feel appropriate to take it.

While this is about listening, it's also about mutual respect; it's not about being a doormat. If you feel they are being too rude, simply and calmly make clear that while you are happy to help as best as you can, if they are being rude you will have to ask them to either call back or change their tone. It's surprising how well this works.

The key here is calm tone. So if you do this, make sure you speak slowly and in a low voice, so as not to enter the battleground.

- *I am really happy to do my very best to help.*

- *However, while I understand you are not happy, your tone and manner is coming across as quite aggressive.*

- *If you'd like me to help, please calm down and I will do my best to assist.*

STEP THREE: EMPATHY AND/OR RECOGNITION

The purpose of this step is to calm them down, show them you are willing to understand, and you are not taking a position of defence or attack. This will literally take the wind out of their sails. If you give them nothing to work with, just the aikido position of using their energy and shifting it, then eventually their energy will just die down and you will be having a normal conversation.

So in this step, all you need to do is tell them that you understand their anger. If you understand why they are angry you can add something like:

- *I understand you are frustrated because...*

- *I understand your values have not been met.*

Another response might be:

- *I totally understand that efficiency is of huge importance to you running this company, and understand that you feel my actions got in the way of that.*

Notice the tone and phrasing: adult, clear and rational. The tone is not submissive or apologetic. Instead, it's about attempting to understand their position, and articulating that you understand. All you are doing here is recognising and acknowledging their problem, giving them space to realise that you will be constructive rather than aggressive.

Under attack, we tend to defend, submit or counter-attack. This way is different. It's stepping away from the war zone, inviting them to a table in another room and suggesting you discuss it like the two adults you are. Now they may come at you with an attack again.

Case study: Handling anger

Client: I am disgusted by the service in your company. I have been treated appallingly, I want a refund and I want to take my business elsewhere.

You need to neutralise the situation. If it's a ball they've lobbed at you, you catch it and hold it, before even thinking about sending it back. Breathe. That's the first thing. Release any tension, so that it doesn't come out in your response. Then you respond.

You: Okay so, I hear you're unhappy at the treatment you've received from the staff here. Is that right? Would you tell me more?

Client: Don't pretend you don't know – you're responsible, too.

That email you signed off, the delay for my records, without an explanation. It's disgusting, Let me speak to the manager!

It's tempting at this point to assert yourself or defend. To say something like:

'I am the manager' or 'fine but they'll say the same thing as me' or 'I'm sorry, please don't shout' or 'Shouting won't get you anywhere'. But none of those will get you anywhere. So better to follow aikido communication rules.

> **You:** I can hear that you have quite a list of things you're not happy with, and I am sorry about that. I need to understand a little more, though. Can you talk me through some of those grievances, and then I'll check back with you that I understand them? To start with, I understand that you are annoyed there was a delay to your records. Is that right?
>
> **Client:** Yes it is right. That's exactly what I said.
>
> **You:** Thanks for clarifying. On that one, I will look into what happened after this call and come back to you when I have found out the exact cause of the delay. But before I do that, are there other grievances you can tell me about?

Please note at this point there is no apology, no taking of responsibility (yet – only when appropriate), just a receiving of the information and some questions. So simple, right? And yet so few people do this.

People like to talk, and they like to be listened to. So if you get your angry client listing their grievances in a way that is safe for them and they feel you are really listening, that is going to take a lot of the sting out of their anger. If you feel tempted to interrupt at any point, to tell them they are wrong or their grievance is unjustified, hold back if you can.

Once they have finished, then it's your chance.

STEP FOUR: SHARING AND TAKING RESPONSIBILITY

Now it depends on your relationship, but the basics always apply whether it's an employee, a client or your superior. Your first sentence after they have finished speaking should include two things: an acknowledgement that you have heard them, and empathy for their situation. Empathy or recognition that their values have not been met is an important step. They can't then tell you you don't understand.

* *I've heard each of your points. I can understand how it must have been really frustrating for you to not receive email notification.*

Finally you get to state your position. Whether you did what you are being accused of, or didn't do it, or have a different perspective altogether, the most important thing is to not step into right and wrong territory. You've come this far, so keep up the excellent aikido! There are three possibilities here.

Simply offer a solution or an action: Offering an action is a simple process. Tell them what you intend to do and in what time frame, then follow up with a question to check in. This is a very powerful way of calming someone.

I will look into it and get back to you by 5pm Tuesday with some responses for each of those points. Does that sound all right?

They have the wrong end of the stick and you now need to explain: If you did not do the thing you are being accused of, then you need to acknowledge their values and ask if you can explain your position. Keep this simple, and maintain your own communication style and space. Keep your voice calm and steady. Don't let their tone of voice and volume grab you unless you do it as a strategic move to build rapport. Own your feelings, but don't state them as objective fact. If their experience is different, then this could annoy them. Instead, keep objective facts and subjective experience separate.

- *There is also another perspective, as we had a different experience on our side. I'd like to share it with you if I may?*

- *I can see why that has appeared like x, and why that would be really frustrating. It was slightly different for me, as .....*

Some kind of acknowledgement will take the wind out of it as they realise you understand and they don't need to fight their position. An honest non-apology could be:

- *I understand that you are really hurt by what happened, or that you're angry because you feel your feelings weren't respected.*

- *However, it feels quite different from my perspective.*

- *I'd like to think about it and maybe we can come to a place where we are both more understanding of each other. Does that sound okay?'*

This is very different from submission, apology or giving in. It is important to choose wording that stays respectful of you and shows understanding for their position, whether you agree with it or not. Remember, explanation can only come after acknowledgment. If you jump in with your side, then you are back to the drawing board. They must know you are not just randomly defending yourself.

You are guilty as charged: If you think you are to blame; take it on the chin. Even if there are extenuating circumstances (and there usually are), then take responsibility.

You can do it whilst still being totally respectful of your own values. Because taking responsibility is respecting their values and owning your actions.

- *I see how my doing x let you down and I apologise for that.*

- *I take full responsibility for the two events and know it is totally unacceptable. It won't happen again.*

Don't make excuses or tell them the reasons why it happened. In our scenario at the beginning of this chapter, she went wrong because she went straight into excuses. Excuses are incredibly frustrating to hear because the individual feels totally unheard, their needs unrecognised.

Sorry

The apology is territory which needs to be negotiated carefully, to maintain personal integrity and to be respectful of another. It is possible to do! Remember, be an advocate of your own and the other person's needs. I know I keep saying it, but I genuinely believe the key to a caring and contented life lies in this powerful statement.

Be sparing with your apologies, not least because there are only two reasons to apologise: for your actions or for their impact on someone's feelings. There is a lot of power play with those words and they need to be handled carefully. Don't apologise unless you need to. Try not to overuse the word sorry or apologise as it can lead to either doormat or insincerity.

Having said that, if you have done something wrong, a simple apology can be the easiest way to defuse the situation. 'I'm so sorry I was late' can just make all the difference. You don't need to lose your power in an apology.

APOLOGISING FOR YOUR ACTIONS

Only do this if you have something to take responsibility for. If you do have something to apologise for, make sure your 'sorry' is clear and specific rather than a vague nod to being wrong. Don't let it be just a word. Rather than just 'I'm sorry', you could say:

- *I realise that I should have told you sooner, that was a mistake and I'm sorry.*

- *I'm sorry if I've made you feel disrespected by doing x. It really wasn't my intention but I can see from your point of view why it might look like that.*

APOLOGISING FOR THEIR FEELINGS

This way can keep you protected but give them a word they sometimes desperately need. It can be used as empathy here, rather than for your own actions. You are delivering empathy for their feelings, understanding for their values and view points, and clarity on your position. *I'm sorry that you feel that way.*

- *I can hear that you are really upset/ frustrated/ angered by this and I'm genuinely sorry about that.*

- *I can see you're hurt and I am so sorry about that. I apologise.*

Apology tip: If you find apologising difficult, try to understand their pain and why they are upset. Build up on empathy. Then your apology can be genuine rather than because you have been backed into a corner.

DON'T APOLOGISE
- Because they want you to.
- When you think it will make your life easier. It just devalues your apology and creates an unhealthy power dynamic.
- If you know someone really wants and apology but you don't feel you have done anything wrong. Don't compromise your integrity.
- When you are backed into a corner; an apology is worthless and slightly shaming. It also leads to resentment and insincerity.
- Just if someone is unhappy with you. As we heard, sometimes values clash, and that's life, it's not your fault.
- For something you didn't do. That undermines your integrity.

But you can apologise for whatever you are genuinely sorry for!

Peaceful communication

When you are ready to speak, watch your tone of voice. If it gets louder, theirs will get louder too. This has been proven in studies with Kenyon Speech Unit many years ago, where they found that we tend to respond to meet the other person's volume. If you refuse to raise your voice, the other person will likely keep their voice reasonable too.

Try to put yourself in their shoes and understand what is going on for them. This will make it much easier not to get caught up in their anger. If you can get to this place where you understand their position, not only will you not get swept up, you will be able to be kind in your responses and show real understanding.

Another useful metaphor for someone's anger is to imagine it is simply an apple: an apple of anger or criticism. When they give it to you, you can hold it calmly, put it down and be curious about it. By doing this, it makes it easier to see it as separate from you. One of the most challenging things with anger

Figure 13.2
If anger were an apple

is to avoid getting caught up in its energy. Remember it is so natural to have fight-or-flight reflexes if someone comes to us angry, but we don't need to believe them. If we wait, objectify their anger, and put it (metaphorically speaking) on the table, it can help us to stay in an adult, neutral place.

How to calm an angry person
/ GOLDEN RULES /

1. Remember to avoid defence and attack and instead practise communication aikido.

2. Breathing helps you move to the cerebral cortex and deal with angry impulses.

3. Whether you agree or disagree with the person attacking, make sure to use empathy and acknowledgment before you state your position.

4. Be careful with the word sorry. It's important you say it with integrity.

5. Remember to be an advocate of your own and the other person's values. That is the way to a peaceful resolution.

Chapter 14 | How to ace at interviews |

In this chapter you will learn about:

- **Getting to know you:** Know your own strengths
- **Is it a good fit:** Are you right for the company? Are they right for you?
- **Matching the skills for the job:** Corresponding skillsets
- **Practical preparation:** Be prepared
- **Excellent performance on the day:** Giving it your best shot at the interview

The ideal interview is for your ideal job, right? It's the job where you are using your skills, where you and your company share the same values, and you communicate well with the people who work around you. The skills I will teach you in this section will help you get any job, but really they are about winning the job that is perfect for you. That's ideal for the employer and ideal for you.

There is a lot of preparation suggested in the next few pages. You might choose to only do the bits that are exciting for you or resonate with you, or you might want to do it all. Whichever you choose, it is important you go into the interview feeling confident and with a clear and uncluttered mind. So please trust yourself though this process and do what feels right for you.

IF WE WERE TO BOIL IT DOWN to its essence, an interview is about one thing and one thing only – how you are going to be the best possible asset to the company in terms of profit margins, the culture and work place – and how they are going to be the best employer for you.

In a good interview, you will need to show how your unique set of skills and characteristics make you great for the job; show your vision and passion for the job; build rapport with the interviewer to make the best impression on the day. To achieve this you need to have two key things down, excellent preparation and excellent performance on the day.

This chapter is therefore made up of those two clear sub-sections. After days of writing the application, followed by days of waiting for a response, the email has finally come through – and to your delight, it's good news. You have an interview in five days. You panic. There is so much you could do. You want the job with a hunger you haven't felt for some time, and yet your free hours over the next few days are limited. Where to begin? Follow the guide below to help you with interview preparation that will get you feeling ready.

As you go through the exercises, make notes so that you can structure and review your preparation.

Getting To Know You

Interviews are largely based on examples of what you have done. People want to get a sense of the real you, and your skillset. If you tell them you have great leadership skills, this will mean nothing to them; it's just words. You have to show them, and you do this through examples. So much of the content preparation of this section is about finding the right kind of examples. In the next section you will be putting them into a STAR structure to ensure that your responses are dynamic and full of important detail.

FIND YOUR VALUES

Figure 14.1
Getting to know you

The place to begin is with your fundamental values. Connecting with your values helps you to be truly authentic in a real and compelling way. Most people start with what the company wants but, while important, that is not the place to start because the company wants to hire YOU. They want to get a real sense of who they are working with.

If you have not worked out your core values, go back to Chapter 10 and do them now, so you will have a record of your six core values.

EXAMPLES OF YOUR VALUES IN YOUR LIFE AND CAREER

Now think of some examples of how you demonstrated those values in your working life, then add the skills you showed in doing so. Here's an example to give you an idea.

I showed creativity when I directed my first play. Half way through the rehearsals I was getting bored of directing the play in the same space, a 17th-century living room. Our theatre space was a big rectangular room, half of which was devoted to the audience, the other half to the set. So I came up with an idea. Make the audience area into a 17th-century garden and in the interval, switch the audience around. So the audience watch the second half of the play from the living room, while it's now performed in the garden. We did it and it was a resounding success.

Skills: lateral problem solving, imagination, leadership.

ARTICULATE YOUR STORY

At some point in the interview, they are likely to ask something along the lines of 'tell me about you'. At this point, you want to make sure you give them a concise and interesting timeline outlining your jobs up until now, what you learnt and your big achievements. They want some idea of what made you you. This needs to be carefully planned so that you are sharing the meat and not the irrelevant detail.

Have you seen Steve Jobs's Stanford Commencement speech? If not, then please take a look[8]. One of the most interesting moments is when he talks about all his life decisions, which made no sense at the time, later becoming part of his rich tapestry. For example, he randomly studied calligraphy, and years later it directly led to their groundbreaking use of artistic fonts for the first Apple computer.

Once you have filled in your own chronological time line, take a look to see if you can spot patterns in your own rich tapestry. You might also like to associate the skills you acquired at each stage in your career, as well as interests, achievements, key turning points and challenges.

EXAMPLES OF YOUR KEY ACHIEVEMENTS AND CHALLENGES

Having done your time line, this next exercise should be pretty easy. I would like you to write down your three to five major achievements or proud moments and three to five challenges or turning points in your life that you feel are most indicative of you. Expand on them in your notes. This will be useful in answering many questions and by doing this thinking now, you get to decide what you share with them.

PRACTISING INTERVIEW QUESTIONS

Once you have done this, have a look at it and, if you can, be objective. Can you see how you have quite a good story?

You now have the basis of your answers to many common interview questions:

*   *Tell us about you.*

*   *What are some of your major achievements?*

*   *Tell us about a big challenge and how you overcame it.*

Practise responding to 'Tell me about you' either with a friend or a voice recorder. See which skills and experiences you want to bring in. It should take no more than five minutes and you should be able to give a good, concise history of your jobs, some of your key achievements and any big turning points or challenges.

Now do the same with other potential questions.

Is It A Good Fit?

Now the next piece is about knowing the kind of company you want to work for. The more you know this, the more clarity you can have in the interview about what you love about the job and the company, and why you should work there.

THE VALUES OF THE COMPANY

At this point, if you have a specific job in mind, go and grab that job description. If you don't, then think of a job title that you would like and intend to go for (or find a job description on the internet that you would love to get).

If you have a job description and details of the company, go through it with a fine-toothed comb. If you don't, have a think about the top five values you would like in a company that you work for, or choose a company you like and admire and research them. Either way, write down five company values, then a description of the skills required for the job that manifest those values.

For example, you might choose:

*   Service: Contribution to society, enriching the world in some way through its work.

*   Growth mindset: Always looking to improve, ways to be better leaders, communicators, provide better service, kind, caring about its staff.

FIND WHERE YOUR VALUES MEET THE COMPANY'S VALUES

We are going to do this by looking at your core values, This time I want you to use them to describe the job you would like. So if a core value is creativity, describe how you would like to be creative in your job role. If a core value is certainty or stability, describe what this looks like in a job – one that is secure with very clear tasks and instructions. I have put an example using my own values below.

Core values: Wise leadership, collaboration, originality, growth, creativity, fun.

A job where I get to lead, but in a way that is about nourishing and developing the people around me. One where I get to be creative, and take time out to develop new ideas, but then have people to collaborate with and bounce off. One where I am constantly learning and growing, and being encouraged to do that as part of my job. One which praises my original thinking and my tangential approach.

Now you have the company value – match it up with your own. For example:

Service: Strong commitment to CSR – matches to my value of Contribution.

Now you can practise relevant interview questions, as you did before, such as:

- *Why do you want to work here?*
- *What do you admire about our company?*
- *What excites you about our company?*

Matching The Skills For The Job

Now we are going to look in more detail at the job itself, identify the skills they are looking for and compare them with the ones you are offering.

THE SKILLS REQUIRED FOR THE JOB

Go through the job description again, and this time look for every task and every skill they mention. If there is a task without a skill, put down what skill you think would be best suited to the task. Five is a good number, but you can do this with any number. If you don't have a specific job you are going for, use an advert for a job you would like, or your ideal job.

Once you have been through in detail, every task they have outlined should be in your job description box, next to a skill. Once you have done this, put a star next to the five most important skills for the job (in your opinion).

Now, taking each skill at a time, justify why that is an important attribute for the role. Try and think about this in terms of the employer. Why is this skill important to them? For example, communication skills are important to get the most out of your team, keep them inspired and motivated and deal well with issues as they arise.

Some skills and qualities you might consider could be:

Calm under pressure, communication skills, computer skills, creative, determination, easy-going, efficient, empathy, entertainer, enthusiastic, fast learner, fixing things, flexibility, good time keeper, good with hands, honest, independent, initiative, lateral thinker, leadership skills, listening skills, maths skills, motivates team, motivational, organizational skills, original thinker, people skills, perfectionist, positive attitude, presentable, problem solver, professionalism, reliable, resourceful, rigour, self-confidence, team player, technical literacy, think on your feet, trustworthy, works independently.

FIND WHERE YOUR SKILLS MEET THE SKILLS REQUIRED FOR THE JOB

Now go back to your list of skills or values. For each word, come up with an example of a time you showed that attribute, quality or skill, such as communication skills or reliability. Can you think of a time that shows you using that skill really well? If so, put it down.

These three steps will massively prepare you for interview questions, and better yet, they will get you to put your own experiences into a framework that will show directly how the company will benefit from having those skills around.

SKILLS YOU WOULD LIKE

Now have a think about three skills that you don't have that you would love. Or areas you would like to grow.

Once you have these down, I want you to look at them a bit closer. I want you to think about the ways in which you do show these qualities in your life, or where and how you have adapted around them. Here's an example for discipline:

When something is really important to me, it gets done. I also exercise most days, although sometimes it's a struggle. I have found that if I really want to be disciplined, I raise the stakes, and that seems to work!

That should prepare you to answer any questions about your weaknesses.

The ideal response to this question is actually around how you manage your weaknesses. This rates you highly on self-awareness and emotional intelligence, important factors that are considered when hiring.

ARTICULATE YOUR VISION

Brilliant. You have done most of your preparation. You should now have a great idea of what you can offer a job, the kind of job you really want, which will be a great match for you in terms of your skills and the kind of company you want to work for. You will also be able to answer most questions. Finally, your vision. This is not an absolute necessity, but is a nice exercise, and prepares you for a couple of questions they might ask you.

I would like you to return to your values list. Describe below what your working life would look like if you were honouring that value to a factor of nine or ten. Place this forward five years in time. Think about how you would be at work if you had that value honoured at ten. What kind of role would you have? Would you be leading or working in a team? Would you be travelling or settled in one place? Would you be challenged or secure? Go for feelings if concrete ideas are eluding you. Imagine yourself as satisfied as you can be with your working life.

Once you have done this, have a read through. Is there a coherent shape? Is this feasible? Could the job you are going for fit with the vision you have outlined? Ask yourself how the job could be part of this vision, and write down how and why.

This will enable you to answer:

*   *Where do you want to be in five years' time?*
*   *What do you see as your career trajectory within this role?*

Practical Preparation

Now we are ready with the meaty prep work, we can get on with the more practical preparation for the day. This includes:

*   Researching the company
*   Preparing your questions for them
*   Selecting your responses to interview questions
*   Using the star structure

RESEARCHING THE COMPANY

It's important you put some time into researching the company – that will mark you out as motivated and doing your job properly. The kinds of things you could look for are:

- Where are they heading?
- What do you think the next five years could look like for the company?
- What will they need in the area of your work to make that growth?
- Who are their competitors?
- What is their USP (unique selling point)?

PREPARE YOUR QUESTIONS FOR THEM

Always have some questions prepared. It shows you take the dynamic seriously and again that you value and respect yourself and your time and want to work for a company that suits you.

Do

- Ask questions that are relevant to the job and to your role and your values.
- Try and link in your questions with research you have done.

For Example:
I read that the company takes CSR really seriously and that is great. Is there scope for getting involved in that side of things as part of my role?

- When you find out about the role, ask if there is career progression in that role.
- Ask for any clarification that you need on the job description.

Don't

- Ask questions that you can easily find the answer to on the internet.
- Ask invasive or presumptuous questions without having built rapport. They might just feel you are nosy. (Why did you set up the company? What is your five-year plan?)

SELECTING YOUR RESPONSES TO INTERVIEW QUESTIONS

Great, the final lap of preparation. If you've got through the above, you are doing really well. The work you have done will not be useful just for interviews but also for getting the most out of a current job, for understanding what makes you tick and building a happy life. By this time you will have a fair few examples and stories. You won't have time to tell them all, but you might well have room for anything from five to ten, depending how long the interview is, so you need to pick the best, plan your responses to classic interview questions, and select which examples you will want to use. You will then put them into what we call the STAR structure, which is a classic way of telling people about yourself in interviews. You can either write this out (recommended) or speak it out into a voice recording device and listen back.

Here we give you some guidelines on where your focus should be when considering your answers.

Tell me about yourself

- They want to hear about your time line, early interests – with an awareness of how they are connected to your interest in the job now.

- Bring out key achievements, challenges or turning points.

- Show how you arrived at where you are now, with your dreams and hopes and aspirations.

Why do you want to work for us?

- This is where you talk about their values and your values aligning.

- Mention what you see as the potential growth for the company and what excites you about that. Explain how you feel you could be important or useful in that area and the satisfaction that would give you.

- Talk about what they do and how you feel you could help.

- Talk about your values and why and how they would be met through this role

Give an example of where you've been able to use your leadership skills

- If you are going for a leadership position then an aspect of leadership should have come up in your various examples. Don't be afraid to go lateral, leadership or team work can encompass all kinds of values and skills, from decisiveness through to positive mental attitude.

What are your key strengths?

- Discuss between three and five of the skills that you have outlined and explain how they relate to the role.

What are your weaknesses?
- Discuss the skills you don't have but want to have.
- Tell them the kind of strategies you employ to ensure you have those skills.

Where do you see yourself in five years?
- They want to know your vision for yourself and see if it matches with theirs. You can talk about how you feel these core values could be met by working in the company.

What is one of your greatest achievements?
- Ensure that the achievement is in line with the skills that you pulled out as central to the job. When you describe the achievement, it should be hitting various skills, again, which are in line with what the job requires. Avoid telling them about an achievement which makes you sound great but has no skill crossover with the role you are interviewing for.

Tell me about coping with a challenge at work or a difficult person in your team
- When you describe the challenge, be sure to show in depth the skills you used to overcome that challenge, and remember to make it personal and take the glory of the positive outcome. (Don't choose a challenge that doesn't have a positive outcome, as you need to show how your skills helped you overcome it.)

Why should we hire you?
- A chance to say how your skills and experience can help grow the organisation and fulfil the duties listed on the job description.

What are your salary expectations?
- Remember what you ask for here is as much a statement of how much you value yourself as it is of how much you want the job. A normal stance is to state what you are getting paid at the moment and that you would expect more as that represents a forward move ment. You shouldn't be accepting the same or less than your most highly paid job to this point, unless there is good reason. At the same time, you must be reasonable, and show self-respect but not arrogance.

What questions do you have for me?

- Use this opportunity to build rapport, referring back to a key point in the inter-view and developing it.

Put it into the STAR structure

Once you have decided which examples you want to use, all examples need to go into STAR structure. This is a structured response to an interview question which supports you to ensure that you don't get lost in irrelevant detail and you focus on the detail that they most need to know.

For each skill or value you are illustrating, organise your information into:

S = situation: Describe the situation that you were confronted with, set the context. Make it concise and informative, concentrating solely on what is useful to the story.

T = task: Explain the particular challenge or task that was required of you.

A = action: This is the most important section as it is where you need to demonstrate your skills and/or values. This means it's good to explain not only what you did, but often how and why you did it. By showing them – not just telling them – you are consciously aware of how your actions will affect the results, you are showing them your skillset.

R = result: Explain what happened as a result of your actions. Also use the opportunity to describe what you accomplished and what you learnt in that situation. This helps you make the answer personal and enables you to high-light further skills. In addition remember:

- Be personal and keep to 'I' not 'we' – they want to know about your achievements, not anyone else's.

- Go into some detail of what you did. The detail makes it real and shows how you operate and gives them a mental picture of how you could be useful for them. Make sure the detail is unique to you and your skillset, though – keep it relevant.

- Steer clear of technical information, unless it is crucial to your story.

Excellent Performance On The Day

Now it's interview time and you want to give yourself the best possible shot. First impressions count. We make decision about someone within the first few seconds of seeing them. The rest of our brains then catch up, creating all kinds of justifications as to why that is. So make a good first impression.

How you show up for the interview is a microcosm of how you work. They will read it as this. Hence, being calm, on time, and looking appropriate are all important signals that you can handle the job. It's obvious, but check the address, preferably the night before, and know the journey and how long it will take and leave plenty of time. Arriving sweaty and flustered and late for an interview is never a good look.

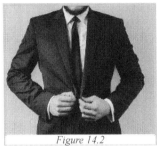
Figure 14.2
What you wear

WHAT YOU WEAR

Your clothes should be in line with you and your own values, and hopefully there is synergy with the company values. If the company values friendliness and you value professionalism, you might find there is a clash in what you should wear. And a clash in values could mean it's not the company for you.

- Get the tone right – and ensure it's going to be in the rough ball park of the company. Which might mean jeans and heels for a PR firm, but definitely not for a bank, or a suit and tie for a bank but definitely not for a film company.

- Avoid any clothes or items that you are not comfortable with, from hair pins to heels to overly tight ties. Make sure your clothes support rather than hinder you.

- Avoid going over-fussy: flowing scarves, handbags dribbling bits and pieces, loads of chunky jewellery. Instead, let you do the talking not your costume. You want to be in control of all the chat, even that of what you are wearing!

- Wear something that is a little unique to you; it will make you feel like you.

WHAT YOU BRING

Bring a spare clean copy of your CV, any downloadable information and any further work you want to show them. Don't have this in a cluster of scrappy papers. Put it in a nice binder. Think through any eventualities. If you are giving a presentation, bring a memory stick with your presentation as a back-up. Don't rely on them.Everything you do will show your level of respect for yourself and your company. They will notice.

MAKING AN ENTRANCE

People will have a sense about you from how you enter, greet them and take your seat, without even knowing why. They will use logic to back up their 'sense', so give yourself every advantage you can so that all your fantastic preparation can do you justice.

Start as soon as you enter the building. Make a good impression on everyone. Smile at the receptionist, say thank you, be polite. Everyone in the building who works there represents the company in some way, they are the eyes and ears. Build rapport with the receptionist or the person who shows you in by smiling, thanking them and, if you like, asking how they are. They could easily be asked for their opinion. If they are, you want them to say how pleasant you were.

If you have to knock on the interview-room door, make it clear and confident, not a hesitant patter. Come in with shoulders back, a smile and eye contact. If there are two or more people, look at each of them and acknowledge them with a smile. They will be waiting for this smile, a sign that this next hour will be good and not painful. Because rest assured, they have likely been doing this for hours and have had enough painful interviews with dead fish, and wan or absent grins or, worse still, clenched jaws and floor-stuck eyes and furrowed brows. They want to like you. Smile or, if that doesn't feel natural, nod and make sure your eyes are warm, and they will feel reassured.

MEETING AND GREETING

Walk forward and offer your hand. Whatever you do, don't let your handshake be limp. The firm handshake says, 'I step in and get involved, I engage with people, I am present.' The limp handshake says, 'here's my hand, you can move it around for a moment and then I'll have it back.' The limp handshake suggests an attitude to life which is passive.

Be firm, but don't squeeze their knuckles to oblivion. The handshake makes a statement of the energy with which you come at things: too weak and it does not bode well; too strong and it can be a bit like a contest!

When you sit down, there is a Goldilocks-style balance to be found. Confidence is good. Arrogance is annoying. You don't want to come in and sit down like you own the place, but you don't want to sit down like you are apologising for being in the room.

Do one thing at a time, go calmly and you won't drop things and fluster. Put down your case or bag, take off your coat, put it at the back of the chair and take your seat. This makes a clear statement: 'I respect myself and I will take the time I need to do something and not fold under pressure.' This is exactly what they want for their company. Someone who is clear headed and self-respecting.

It's been all of 20 seconds so you are still in first-impression zone. If they offer you water or a drink, take it with a clear thank you. Let your eyes be alert and your smile be genuine. Let your arms rest on the table or on your lap – do not cross them. Be aware of your posture, keep your body open, and no curved shoulders or slumping. If you slump, it's as if the invisible string holding you together isn't working and you are broken or disconnected somewhere in the middle. It will affect your voice (as your breath won't get all the way to your diaphragm).

These first moments are the jungle equivalent of being sized up and sizing up the other cat. They may be in a position to hire you, and to potentially change your life in the desired direction, and yet this is not about giving them the power. This is about showing them how useful you can be to them, and how you feel your value will add value to their company. So do not lose your status. Be respectful of yourself at all times!

BUILDING RAPPORT

They will most likely start by asking you a rapport-building question. Answer to build rapport, not for the answer. And you can ask a question back like 'How's your day been so far?' if it feels appropriate. In all the interviews I have held as an interviewer (and there have been many over the years I have been running my own business), I have hardly ever been asked a question back, but when I have, it was so nice I instantly responded and warmed to the interviewee in the process.

In terms of your pace and speaking style, you want to be in the ball park of their tone, pace and volume. If they are hammering out questions and not smiling, you will find it easier to build rapport if you are talking at a similar speed. This is something you will probably be doing automatically to some extent, but it's good to be aware of. So meet them around where they are at. I have not hired people because they were talking so loudly in the interview I felt bombarded. I run a communication company so I am wanting to hire people who are able to intuitively do this, but the same thing goes. If you have an interviewer who is talking very softly and you are speaking at a high volume, this may put them off, even if they don't realise it.

RESPONDING TO QUESTIONS

Take your time: Be prepared to take time to answer their questions. Ensure that you don't rattle on with a casual answer because of nerves but instead take the time you need to come up with the considered response. If that means pausing to find the right word or idea, then do so. You can also jot down a couple of points at the beginning of their questions. If this helps you be succinct, then they will know you know how to manage yourself so you perform at your best. Many people tend to rush into answers, but actually giving yourself time to consider it makes a subtle statement about respecting your own needs. This also creates a healthy power dynamic, rather than the interviewer batting the question ball and the interviewee running wherever it's been sent to fetch it.

Measure your pace: Use pauses. It's really important you don't drown them in a story, but that you talk steadily, letting them keep pace with you, delivering your units and ideas. Remember, they have probably seen a few people before you and have a few to go, and speaking to someone who doesn't deliver their ideas but pours out words like they're going out of fashion, can be painful and exhausting.

Enjoy telling your stories: They should all be nicely structured STAR examples, with a clarity on the meaty bits that best show your skills. Let yourself be the master storyteller here. Make sure you know the key points in each STAR story, and slow down over these, putting colour and energy into those phrases and words.

Maintain a good structure: Follow the STAR structure. It also can be very good to start a response to a question by preparing them with what you are about to say. A little like an intro sentence when writing an essay. If you have a number of examples or points to make in response to their question, mention the number, before giving the points. This will make them feel in very safe hands and also show that you are well prepared and have an organised mind. For example:

How could the company benefit from having you?

Well, I feel there are three key ways in which the company would benefit from having me in this role. My organisational ability, my managerial skills, and my marketing experience. Is it okay if I give you a bit of background on each of these?

Leave on a high: At the end of the interview, thank them for their time, wish them well for the rest of the day, smile and give a strong handshake (not necessarily in that order).

That's it. If you get all of this in, then if the job is a good fit for you, and you are a good fit for the job, you will have put nothing in the way of you getting it. You will be succinct, prepared, with strong responses that clearly show your skills and are backed up by evidence. You will come across as friendly, confident, at ease, and respectful of them and yourself with good communication skills. And most of all, you will be authentic. So get preparing for the job of your dreams!

How to ace at interviews
/ GOLDEN RULES /

1. Take the time you need to prepare your responses; it will be worth it.

2. Do the Values exercise. It can be a game changer.

3. Research the company thoroughly and come with questions and a sense of their values and USP. You'd be surprised how many people don't take the time to do this.

4. Be efficient – know where you are going, what to take with you, and plan your journey so you get there in plenty of time.

5. Enjoy the process, talk to them and build rapport, and relax. Once you have done the hard preparation work, as long as you don't slump in your chair, you can let it unfold.

Chapter 15 | Mastering powerful presentations |

In this chapter you will learn about:

- **Content:** Defining your objective
- **Structure:** Shaping your presentation
- **Non-verbal communication:** Words are just the start
- **Common pitfalls:** And how to avoid them

Far too many people find the prospect of giving a presentation daunting, or even terrifying. And equally far too many people dread sitting in presentations because of dull, lengthy speeches that leave the listeners none the wiser. Yet presentations are a huge part of what so many of us do. In this section, you will discover the key skills and tools you need to have in order to give engaging, effective presentations. You will also learn what you must avoid in order to prevent your presentations from nose-diving into a presentation hell hole.

Scenario: What John did wrong

John is assistant vice president and is talking about the latest figures. He is attractive, warm and a popular member of the team. He stands up in the room of 20 to do a 30-minute presentation. You like John and are interested in what he is working on. But as he stands shuffling his notes, not making eye contact, trying to find the right page, you feel your mind wandering. He starts speaking, reading through the slides, with his back mostly turned towards the people in the room as he does so.

Every so often he glances back at the room, sending the odd look in the direction of his audience. He reads in a monotone, in long sentences, with complex thoughts that are barely differentiated.

Try as you might, your eyes get heavy, you find yourself thinking about the argument you had with your wife as you left home this morning. John finishes and asks if anyone has any questions. People look down and shuffle their own papers, the room is filled with mutters and people reading hurriedly through the slides. People file out of the room, and you find yourself dragging your feet, dreading the day ahead.

What did John do wrong? Firstly, his presentation content lacked gripping potential. There was no structure, and his sentences were long and tedious. Secondly, the way he spoke was lacklustre – there was no colour in his voice, no delivery, pausing, emphasis, all the things we know to be important! Thirdly, his body language and eye contact were virtually non-existent, so along with his monotonous voice there was nothing to grip onto. Remember the vocal landscape metaphor? Well, his was a barren land. Finally, he hadn't thought about why he needed to speak to these people beyond being told to, so his motivation wasn't clear and he felt insincere.

Content

We want to engage our audiences, whether it's a pitch about how your company's drill will work more efficiently than others or an information-based presentation about how studying twins can impact developing countries.

FOCUS ON PERSONAL VALUES

Figure 15.1
Superman

Superman stood for truth and justice and we loved him for it. If you can bring your values into your speech, even if it is in a small and subtle way, it can be much more impactful. You can win people's hearts and minds, because they get to see your passion, what makes you tick. It might be your personal journey, why you are interested in your subject or which values are being met in the project. Whatever it is, a bit of you goes a long way. If you haven't yet established your values, look at Chapter 10.

Use of story

If you can find a way to use some story in your presentation, it will pay dividends. Find a character or a client who exemplifies the point you are wanting to make, and put their story into a simple five-act structure shown below. (You can also shorten it to three acts – problem or challenge, action and solution, conclusion, resolution and evidence.)

DID YOU KNOW?

EVIDENCE OF THE POWER OF STORIES

In the first ad (A) they told the story of Rokia (see below). In the second ad (B) they made it faceless.

Ad A

Rokia, a seven-year-old girl from Mali, Africa, is desperately poor and faces the threat of severe hunger or even starvation. Her life will be changed for the   better as a result of your financial gift. With your support, and the support of other caring sponsors, Save the Children will work with Rokia's family and other members of the community to help feed her, provide her with education, as well as basic medical care and hygiene education.

Ad B

• Food shortages in Malawi are affecting more than 3 million children; in Zambia, severe rainfall deficits have resulted in a 42% drop in maize production from 2000. As a result, an estimated 3 million Zambians face hunger; four million Angolans – one third of the population have been forced to flee their homes; more than 11 million people in Ethiopia need immediate food assistance.

Ad A was more than 100% more successful, with people donating about one and a half times as much as through B.

Ad A donations – $2.83 on average
Ad B donations – $1.16 on average

STRUCTURING YOUR STORY

There is a well-known five act structure which is often used to shape film and TV storylines. It is useful to hook the listener or audience in, and keep them engaged. The idea is that through going on a journey with the protagonist, the audience becomes invested in the outcome. It's a great structure to be mindful of when writing or telling a story in a presentation or a speech, and while it can mean doing some simple tweaks to the order of the story, the effect can lead to a powerful increase in audience engagement. Very useful then to have the structure to hand! Have a look at the classic five act structure below.

DID YOU KNOW?

Five Act Structure

Act one: The exposition

Here, the audience learns the setting (time/place), characters are developed, and a conflict is introduced.

Act two: Rising action

The action of this act leads the audience to the climax. It is common for complications to arise, or for the protagonist to encounter obstacles.

Act three: The climax

This is the turning point of the play. The climax is characterised by the highest amount of suspense.

Act four: Falling action

The opposite of rising action, in the falling action, the story is coming to an end, and any unknown details or plot twists are revealed and wrapped up.

Act five: Denouement or resolution

This is the final outcome of the drama. Here the authors' tone about his or her subject matter is revealed, and sometimes a moral or lesson is learned.[9]

WHAT DO YOU WANT TO ACHIEVE?

Next, you need to connect with the objective of your presentation. What is the best possible outcome? To answer this, think about what effect you want to have on your audience. What do you want to make them come away feeling. Inspired? Delighted? Excited or motivated? Do you want them to buy the product or change their life in some way? Get really clear on the change you want to effect in your listener, the new understanding you want them to have. The way in which whatever you're talking about will make their or someone else's lives better (usually this is the case – by the fact there is a problem to be solved).

While there will be some large overall objectives, for a longer presentation, each section of the presentation is likely to have smaller mini objectives, and these will need to also have a structure – problem, solution, evidence, summary.

Structure

There is a straightforward structure that suits most presentations and has proved to be successful. You can vary it to suit the presentation but, whatever the topic, it should be well shaped into a logical sequence: problem, solution, evidence, summary.

PROBLEM

This might be a problem for your audience or a problem you are trying to get your audience to engage with. Whatever it is, there is usually a problem. It can be told in a story form, or a case study with a powerful hook. The more story you can use, the better. You can also bring in your own motivation in terms of solving the problem, why it interests you, which values of yours it is meeting. Again, it helps to have a personal aspect to engage people. It could simply be that when you heard about the problem you wanted to be part of the solution.

SOLUTION

This could be a quick fix, or a longer, more academic information piece, but it should offer your solution. Ensure you show how the solution works and specifically how the solution will address their problem and the consequences of their problem. This is the time to be an expert. Values can also be mentioned here.

The more you number and structure and map it out, the more people will be able to grasp the material. For example:

We have identified five key components here and will be focusing most of our attention on the following three ... Now, beginning with the first of these over here, it is made up of seven aspects, each with its own..... .

As much as possible, link the solution back to the problem and, if you can, some references to the story. This helps make it tangible.

Keep your sentences short, try not to overload one sentence with too many complex terms.

Keep it relevant to the interests of your audience. For example, if you were presenting to an audience of pensioners, you might push the safety aspect, whereas if you were presenting to an audience of teenagers, you might be pushing the excitement factor. Now that is simplistic, and I expect your genuine situations will be much more complicated, but the main point is, think about what your audiences want rather than what you want, and your solution should be responsive to that.

EVIDENCE

Whether it's a pitch or information, here is where you offer the evidence to back up your point – previous success cases, how well the solution has worked in the past – to establish trust and credibility. Evidence is needed so an individual can make decisions with both their head and their heart. Evidence usually appeals to the head, so include statistics that prove your case. The heart is usually more satisfied with stories and values – do they like you? do they trust you? do they want to help you? – so keep relating your evidence to your objective and your values. The idea is that you provide all they need to make a decision through their heart (through presentation skills, delivery and rapport) and make sure that their head has what it needs to back it up.

SUMMARY

Finish with a brief concluding summation of their problem and why you believe you can help. This is a time to mention values to round off your presentation.

Non-Verbal Communication

Being aware of your body language is crucial to an effective presentation. You can add so much to your presentation with your posture, stance, entrance, gesture and facial expression, and by the same note, you can take away just as much (or more) if your body is not saying what you want it to say.

TAKING YOUR SPACE

Find your position on the stage and take a first moment to connect with the audience. This can be a smile, or simply looking at them and giving a nod. This can help in a couple of ways. It shows you really taking your space, rather than rushing in to the presentation. It's a moment to reconnect you to the objective of your presentation or speech, which is to share some information with these people. This can be an excellent way to deal with nerves and come back to the human connection that is at the centre of good communication.

Stand firmly and use the floor to ground you; it can help you feel anchored and confident. Ensure your posture is upright and your shoulders are back and down. For more on this see Chapter 4.

EYES IN PRESENTATIONS

Let's assume you don't know your presentation by heart, so you will need to do some reading from slides or paper during the presentation. With that in mind, you clearly can't make constant eye contact and why would you want to? Remember, with eye contact, it's not about quantity, but quality.

The place to make your 'quality' eye contact is at the end of your sentences or at the end of an important point. This makes a psychological statement to your audience; that you really want them to receive and understand this point, thereby making them feel important. The common mistake is to look up in the middle of sentences, which gives the impression you are checking if people are still listening. Not the best impression to make!

If you need a reminder, go over the information in Chapter 8.

CONNECTION SPACES FOR PRESENTATIONS

Connection spaces will be a great help to building shape and dimension in your presentation, helping you to make it stick in people's minds and differentiate one part from another. There are a couple of ways to do it. Go through your presentation asking yourself which connection space is most appropriate for each section; or what the goal is for the audience for each section: what do you want them to feel? Fascinated, excited or curious? Then match it to the connection space that feels most appropriate. You might use intimate to build intrigue, performance to excite, relaxed to make people feel at ease.

To read more about connection spaces, go back to Chapter 6.

HOW YOU SAY IT

Use the intonation technique to make the presentation sound great. For more detail, go to Chapter 3.

- Read through your presentation underlining key words or phrases that represent big ideas that you want to get across. There should be a few on each slide.

- Insert breaks into your speech or divide your thoughts up into smaller units.

- Practise reading out loud and let yourself make each unit interesting. Put attention into getting your underlined words or phrases into the heads of your listeners.

- Deliver to your audience using eye contact. Imagine your ideas are like £10 notes you are putting into the hands of people in the audience.

Common Pitfalls

There are some big pitfalls in presentations. Follow the positives and avoid these negatives and you'll be doing really well!

A weak opening: Shuffling papers, fiddling with screen, dealing with technical problems, an incoherent opening line.

Statements that lose you credibility: I hope this isn't boring, I put this together quite last minute, I'm not really an expert on this but …

Complicated jargon: You are aiming to communicate, not confuse.

Waffling: It's not about counting the words but making the words count.

Lack of structure: If your presentation wanders, so will the attention of your audience.

Poor body language: Slumping, pacing, shuffling, hands in pockets, back to the audience, curved shoulders, crossed arms.

Lack of eye contact: Or not making eye contact to coincide with your crucial points.

Technical problems: Make sure you know what facilities will be available. You will probably be using your laptop so test everything and have the cables needed to link to a projector.

But don't rely on the technology to do a brilliant presentation – have clear notes, a print-out of your slides, and be prepared to talk it through. If technology lets you down, start with a strong statement so they get a good first impression.

Overwhelming the audience: Don't give the audience too much information or overwhelm them with irrelevant detail.

Over-reliance on the slides: Reading from the slides is the worst possible thing you can do. Use the slides as visual teasers, or reminders of your points, but remember – you are giving the presentation, and are the person who will make it sink or swim. So use your slides to add value, but don't expect them to be the value!

Scenario: What Mary did right

Mary comes into the room; she has a sheaf of papers and a confident, efficient air. You were there last time when Mary presented on the latest project and it didn't go so well, she was clearly nervous and you'd felt worried for her for the entire time, so you've been a little apprehensive about the next hour ahead of you. But this time, it feels different.

She walks to the front of the room, places her papers down on the table in front of her, nods, smiles, and says good morning to the people in the room. She seems to be taking time to really connect with people, making eye contact and acknowledging everyone. You notice that everyone in the room stirs and turns towards her, giving her their full attention. Already this is unusual.

She begins her presentation. It is short and to the point, she makes lots of eye contact, her voice is light and pleasant to listen to, her sentences clear and her slides easy to understand. At the end, there's a bubbly energy in the room, people asking questions, curious and engaged.

You realise the whole presentation went in, people absorbed it. And with greater surprise, you enjoyed every minute of it. You're not quite sure what she did, it seemed effortless, but you know it worked. 40 minutes later, you leave the room, your head buzzing with how you can incorporate her proposal into your projects. On your way out, you stop her. 'Mary, that was great. Different from before. How did you...?' Your voice trails off. It seems wrong to ask, like it would admit weakness or something. So you never found out what Mary did. Well, you've come to the right place. Mary read this book.

WHAT DID MARY DO RIGHT?

Content: Her content was simple, well structured and relevant. She used the four rules of content for presentations. Result? She hooked people's attention and held it.

How she said it: She used the intonation technique so her voice had colour and her pace worked for her listeners. She delivered her ideas to the listeners using tone and eye contact.

Non-verbal: She used gesture to animate her presentation and further articulate her points. She used three of the four connection spaces, giving her presentation further dimensions.

Principle of authenticity: She relied on the principle of authenticity to make sure that her presentation had meaning for her.

Mastering powerful presentations
/ GOLDEN RULES /

1. Make sure that your content includes story and, if possible, some personal motivations or values. This will help build engagement with the audience.

2. Use a structure in your presentation to give it shape and use some numbers or mapping so people are very clear where they are and which point you are on.

3. Try the connection space as a tool to give your presentation physical dimension and range.

4. Make sure you deliver your ideas to the audience, using eye contact and body language, rather than turning your body to the slides.

5. Let the first moment be a powerful one by connecting to the audience and grounding using the floor.

Chapter 16 | Delivering inspiring public speeches |

In this chapter you will learn about:

- **Writing the speech:** Spend time on your content
- **Practising the speech:** To make it sound effortless
- **Delivering the speech:** And deserving the applause

A speech reminds us that words, like children, have the power to make dance the dullest beanbag of a heart.

Peggy Noonan

A great speech has the power to turn the world on its axis, to inspire, motivate and even brainwash huge numbers of people. It's amazing what a collection of words and sounds, combined with someone's energy and intention, can do. We look around us and see the evidence of human creation, in motorways and skyscrapers, railways and vast underground tunnels. How many grand speeches were the first step to igniting the course of events that led to these creations? Probably hundreds. Then you have the speeches behind other world events: politics, war. At the time of writing, politics in Britain and America has been like a whirling dervish of activity, and all the while, voters pulled in different directions, swayed or convinced by speeches delivered by the people fighting for their ideas to become manifest.

So why do speeches hold such power? It's a heady mix of brilliant storytelling and someone's passion, belief and message being channelled through their body, voice and words that can stretch out to knock listeners off their feet.

MOST OF US WON'T GET THE OPPORTUNITY to make a speech that has potentially world-changing impact. However, it's likely all of us will need to make a speech or two in the journey of a lifetime, and therein lies an opportunity to light up someone's mind with thoughts they've never had before. A hobby can take you into speech territory, certain jobs can propel you towards it, or if you do charity work you may have to stand upand speak. Out of all the opportunities to make speeches, it is probably weddings and funerals that most of us, at some point in our lives, will need to commit to. They also exert a pressure to be both humorous and sensitive, warm and meaningful. No mean feat when you couple that with inexperience, reluctance and, for many, terror at the prospect! So where do we begin?

Well first, let's try to generate some excitement. Putting the fear of public speaking aside, (and if you've read the chapter on fear you know that public speaking is second only to the fear of dying for a huge number of people), the opportunities a speech offers are vast. Giving a speech gives you a chance to share something of your heart, your passion, your world view, with an audience. An opportunity to hold the attention of anything from a small group to hundreds of thousands of people, and make them feel as you do. And that's an opportunity worth doing well. You need to write a speech you believe in, practise it to get the delivery compelling and the speech firmly in your mind and then communicate it with style. We'll help you with all three.

Figure 16.1
Writing the speech

Writing The Speech

The blank page compels you, or perhaps taunts you – where do you start? Here are some ideas for writing a speech worth saying.

Start by going through these headings and jotting down notes and ideas. Don't expect the speech simply to flow from your pen or keyboard. You will need to keep adding, taking away and reorganising as you work through the process.

YOUR OBJECTIVE

The first thing to do is to decide your objective. What do you want to achieve with your speech? If you have a clear objective in mind, then you can keep a check on whether your speech is following it or deviating from it. You can make sure that every point is in some way aiming or building up to your overall objective.

YOUR TONE

The second thing to understand is the effect you want to have on your audience; this will help you decide the tone of your speech. You might want to make them laugh at one point, love you in the next, be inspired in the next point and sign up on the final one. Whatever it is, make some overall decisions about this, as it will help you to write and then, as you write, you can be more specific.

YOUR PASSION

Thirdly, passion. Whatever the speech is about, it needs to be of genuine interest to you. You need to care about it if you want other people to care too. This means you need to find the idea which engages you, the action you want people to take or the message you want to share, how you want them to feel and why. When you have this clear in your head and heart, you are off to an excellent start.

USE ANECDOTE

You may now have a rough outline of the purpose of your speech and your message. It's time to start thinking of some stories. Delve into your memory bank (or do some research) to find some compelling stories to share. Personal stories are the best, as they help people to truly connect with you and your reason for speaking. If the audience can imagine a protagonist and connect with them, the speech is halfway there. Michelle Obama, who is quickly becoming recognised for her powerful speeches and communication skills, is a pro at sharing her personal story in a way that builds empathy and engagement, and shows her heart.

Think of a good wedding speech you have heard. Usually it will have some stories of the bride or groom and various misadventures. The use of story is key to making it interesting and helping people connect.

BIG THEMES

It might be that your message or purpose is automatically a big one, or perhaps it is a sweet ode to someone you care about. Whatever it is, if you want your speech to have impact on a large number of people, then you need to connect it to some bigger themes – themes that can resonate with everyone. These are universal ideas or values, ones that people intuitively understand and which evoke an emotional response in everyone. For example: justice or love, freedom or knowledge, patriotism or gratitude. If you can combine inspirational ideas or issues that involve all of us with a story, then you have a formula for really engaging your audience. By sharing your story, people can connect with you, and by linking it to bigger themes, they can connect it to themselves. Oscar speeches are a good example. If they are too self-absorbed they are cringeworthy, and if they are too detached they are tedious.

Look at the words of Nobel Peace Prize winner Kailash Satyarthi in his TED talk in response to the question: Who or what inspires you and why?

Each time when I free a child, (I am inspired by) the child who has lost all his hope that he will ever come back to his mother, the first smile of freedom. And the mother who has lost all her hope that her child will come back and sit in her lap, her first tear of joy rolls down on her cheek. I see the glimpse of God in it, and that is my biggest inspiration. And I am so lucky that not once but thousands of times I have been able to witness my God in the faces of those children. And they are my biggest inspiration.

His response is vast, but also so personal it becomes incredibly moving.

While this is more relevant to a public speech with a mission than a family-orientated situation such as a wedding or a funeral, you still have the option to link to bigger themes, even if you are talking at a family occasion of that kind. After all, love and death are pretty much up there in terms of human experiences.

The themes you choose can be simple or complex, but usually they are about what it means to be human and, within that, the struggles and triumphs involved, in equality, justice, peace, love, fragility, gratitude.

Figure 16.2
Malala giving a speech

Another great example is the speech of Malala Yousafzai, Pakistani activist for female education and the youngest-ever Nobel Prize winner, to the UN in 2013, in which she moved from her personal experience to bigger themes that resonated with everyone.

The terrorists thought they would change my aims and stop my ambitions. But nothing changed in my life except this. Weakness, fear and hopelessness died. Strength, power and courage was born.

Each time she moved from her experience to a larger human experience, she was greeted with thunderous applause. Her final words stated a theme and a rallying cry with universal appeal.

We believe in the power and strength of our words. Our words can change the whole world because we are all together, united for the cause of education.

BE AUTHENTIC

The most important thing when writing a speech is that you are sharing something of yourself. Don't try to write a clever speech – you will be much better off to write a speech that genuinely means something to you. It can be scary revealing yourself like this, but it's this kind of content that makes a speech moving.

OPENING

It could be that the opening is the last thing you complete because it is important to get it just right. Keep going back to it until you are happy that you can't improve it. If you can, open your speech with a hook. You want to capture people's attention in that first moment or two, so make that first line powerful. Is it a question? An image? A story? Whatever it is, the more you build some intrigue and engagement in those first moments of your speech, the more the audience feel they are in the hands of an expert, and are engaged and receptive from the start.

Practising The Speech

It usually takes more than three weeks to prepare a good impromptu speech.

Mark Twain

Practice is essential when delivering a speech. You need to find the rhythm, the dull bits, the funny bits. A great speech will go through several edits to be honed down to a polished version. Ideally you want to arrive at a distilled version of what you are saying, so each line is there for a reason, and every part of the speech has a value.

This practice is about really understanding your message, and ensuring that your performance and your non-verbal communication tells the story and adds to the story, too. In order to shape it, and make sure it is as powerful and engaging as it can be, I recommend really taking time to go through the speech and find the journey that you can articulate with your voice and body.

SEVEN STEPS TO PRACTISING YOUR SPEECH

STEP ONE

Remind yourself of your overall objective and what, for you, is the best possible outcome of this speech. As you read through the speech, following the steps below, make sure you feel you are in line with this.

STEP TWO

Write out the speech and then break it up in terms of structure. Each key structure moment will have a number of important points you want to make. Write those out as bullet points.

STEP THREE

Read through the speech and look for key words or phrases that feel particularly important or even that you particularly like. Highlight these literally with a highlighter pen. Later you will be highlighting these with your voice (for more on this see Chapter 3). Once you have done this, mark out little pause points after big ideas. This is where you will be connecting to your audience through eye contact. (for more on this see Chapters 3 and 4).

STEP FOUR

You can now do a couple of practice runs. This can be done somewhere private, but make sure you are clear where your audience is. Focus on the key points you want to deliver to your audience. Underline these. Having a handful of those important moments in your muscle memory will help ground you when you actually deliver the speech for real, and it will connect you with your overall objective.

STEP FIVE

Whilst practising, you will hopefully have been aware of different energy opportunities at various points. This will be where you move from one connection space to another. You might find it easier to think about it as slightly different mini objectives for each section. By marking out different connection spaces in your speech, you will ensure there is a range of gestures, and it keeps things interesting (for more on this see Chapter 6).

STEP SIX

For your notes, make bullet points into single words that act as all the reminders you need. You should be avoiding superfluous points. If a point doesn't fit within a clear objective, then you would be wise to consider dumping it. Having one or two of those points will be okay. Any more, and there's a danger your audience will get lost.

STEP SEVEN

Once you have your broad structure, your bullet points and your single words, you can have a good sense of the shape of your speech. That should be on a card, and the card can be there as your trigger. Now you can practise for real. You can do this in the privacy of your home, but it will be good (particularly if the speech is important) if you can deliver it to one or two others. When delivering it to your stand-in audience, take notice of when they seem engaged and when they seem not so engaged. Ask them at the end for specific feedback about their levels of engagement at different points. Also ask what they got out of it, and see if that aligns with your objectives.

Delivering The Speech

Look back through the earlier chapters and focus on the areas where you know your natural talents need a little help.

THE ENTRANCE

As we know from the chapter on posture, first impressions count, so the way you walk onto the stage matters. Let your shoulders be back, your head upright and your chin level. If you can, smile and make eye contact with your audience. Have a firm step, and take your space with confidence – or at least the appearance of confidence even if you are quaking slightly inside!

When you stand, take a moment before you start speaking to just absorb your space. This will ground you in the room and let the audience see you and you see them. It's a subtle thing, but in this moment you can start to build a connection with your audience that will be fortified as you carry on. Always keep in mind: they want you to do well and be engaging, so they can be engaged! Most of all, they want some authenticity, so remember that.

DELIVERY

As we know from the first section of this book, you have to deliver your idea to your audience. They need to receive your message! So you are going to use your voice, your gesture and, most of all, your eye contact to do this. Use the tools from Chapters 3, 4, 6 and 7 to give you the tools for this. Remember, try to avoid the temptation of looking down at your notes at the end of a sentence. Instead, make sure that you get the big ideas out and make eye contact with them. Remember this is sustained eye contact with the audience on those final words of a sentence (see Chapter 4 for more detail on this). Speak steadily, and with colour in your voice.

Public speaking and the five principles

Authenticity: Be yourself and make it personal. Share yourself with your audience - a real piece of you with real feeling. Your real gift to them. Your vulnerability, your passion.

Connect with your audience: Connecting is about getting past the layers of 'stuff' which can make us forget who we are and what matters, to the beating hearts beneath. A speech can be thought of as a conversation, an exchange of energy. You achieve this by really caring about what you are saying, and really caring about them hearing it. It's that simple.

Commitment and passion: Find your passion, your 'why'. If the speech has your 'why' in it, and you share it fully, it will be compelling. Once you have your 'why', commit wholeheartedly to the telling of it. Do what it takes to share your message. Be prepared to go to gear four or five.

Courage: It is natural to find public speaking a bit scary. But take courage and then connect deeply with your message and your desire to share it through connection with the audience. They are simply individuals - receptive, captive and wanting the gift you are about to share, even if they don't know it yet. So breathe deeply and go for it.

Integrity and purpose: Stand up with the integrity of claiming your space in the world, your right to speak and your voice. Let your spine be straight. You have a message to share. That is all you need.

APPLAUSE

When you have finished, make eye contact with the audience, smile and let the applause begin. Accept that moment fully and absorb it. This is the audience speaking to you, this is their part of the conversation, so let them finish and feel listened to, as they listened to you. The applause is their statement that they have been engaged, received the gift and appreciate it. So don't rush past this moment. Ride it like the crest of a wave.

Figure 16.3
Charlie Chaplin

DID YOU KNOW?
Charlie Chaplin's Speech

In the film, The Great Dictator, Charlie Chaplin made a tremendous speech which illustrates so much of the above. In this speech, after a few lines, we forget it is a script, as his trembling conviction and emotion take over. His voice tremors, his eyes pierce, his gestures show us that he is swept up in what he is saying. It is his courage in revealing his emotional connection to what he is saying that makes this speech electrifying.[10]

Here are 10 reasons why it is so powerful:

1. His pace is speedy and gathers momentum, giving the sense he is captured by the passion of the moment.

2. His voice filled with pathos.

3. His tone modulates, energy bristles through the speech and we can feel it gathering.

4. It is emotional but not indulgent.

5. The words are so intense that he does not need to play them hard.

6. Three minutes into the speech and his body is alive, his shoulders juddering with energy.

7. His eye contact hits its target.

8. He is talking as if this is his only chance to get the message across and he is saying it to people he has to get in touch with.

9. There is no lethargy, no apathy, no half presence.

10. His message is clear, powerful and universal.

Speak as if you are fully committed to changing the audience with your words. That's what incredible speakers have in common.

Delivering inspiring public speeches
/ GOLDEN RULES /

1. Balance your personal story with bigger themes for a truly powerful speech.

2. Commit yourself to practise, to distilling the speech so it is honed and powerful, for the maximum impact.

3. Deliver your speech using the techniques of this book: real eye contact, pauses, and colour in your voice.

4. Connect with your audience from the moment you enter the stage.

5. Remember the principles, be prepared to step up, show your true self, have courage, and deliver your message with power – and your speech will be a hit.

PART 4

Classic elocution techniques

Chapter 17 | You can learn beautiful enunciation |

In this chapter you will learn about:

- **Blunting our consonants:** The three ways we do it
- **How to practise:** The principles to follow
- **Vocal warm-up:** Getting your equipment in gear
- **Finding your intention:** Nothing should get in the way of your message
- **Mixed consonant diagnostics:** Making specific improvements
- **Tongue twisters:** Practise particularly pertinent problems

Most of the tools in this book will help you with speaking well, but elocution is where it gets a little more specific, because now we are looking at the actual sounds you are making, how these sounds are enunciated and where, if anywhere, you are going amiss. For those of you who want to speak in a more formal way, or who have a regional accent you would prefer to soften, or if you are someone who mumbles, this chapter will help you achieve those goals and more. If you are doing a public speech and want to limber up your vocal instrument, then head straight for the vocal warm-up section, which will help you sound crisp and clear.

IF, AT THE END OF THE CHAPTER, you feel you are just getting started, then the next steps is to work with a trained coach, who can diagnose exactly where you are and plan a route to where you want to get to.

Blunting Our Consonants

The focus here is on clear enunciation and, specifically, focusing on clear consonants. As we know from the word power section, consonants are crucial to defining your ideas and delivering them with impact. But many of us are guilty of mistreating and there are three clear pitfalls we will focus on here: mumbling, dropping T's and D's, and mixing up consonants. All of which is to the detriment of good communication. So let's crack it!

PITFALL ONE: MUMBLING

When a speaker lacks muscularity and mumbles, this is often about a lack of solid consonants.

Imagine, if you will, a drunk person, slurring his words while shouting at the top of his voice. How many crisp consonants can you hear? Not many! His tongue is thick with alcohol and dehydration. He might seem to care a lot about what he is saying, but certainly not enough about us understanding.

The mumbler is on a less extreme end of this spectrum. It could be fogginess in the mouth; it could be he simply doesn't open his mouth enough. Whatever it is, there are not many sharp consonants around. Which means, of course, we cannot hear the words clearly. And if you can't clearly hear words, powerful communication is well nigh impossible.

Mumbling can also be viewed as a get-out clause from committing to your ideas and communicating your message. As the mumbler doesn't articulate properly, it suggests they are not so bothered about their ideas getting across.

The remedy: If you have a lazy tongue making fleeting contact with other bits of your mouth in order to emerge with some vague semblance of sounds, then you need to get in there and kick that tongue into gear! If your tongue doesn't have the energy to make proper contact with the roof of your mouth, then it's time for a sergeant major type to yell the equivalent of 'on the floor, ten press-ups NOW!'. Which in mouth speak is – vocal warm-up.

Do five to ten minutes a day of a selection of the vocal warm-up, choosing at least one exercise from each of the three stages.

PITFALL TWO: DROPPING TS AND DS

When I was growing up, I was told to 'pronounce my Ts and Ds' by parents enthusiastic that I should be 'well spoken'. While at the time I found it embarrassing, I now appreciate where they were coming from. It turns out, though, that they were only partially correct. To sound well spoken, you don't need to pronounce every consonant. If you drop consonants that are in the middle of a thought, then most of the time it doesn't really matter because most people won't notice.

However, as mentioned earlier, there are two occasions on which you really do hear a dropped consonant: in the middle of a word – like bu-er (butter) or at the end of a thaw… I mean thought. This is where you will want to pick up those consonants in order to have more power over your speech.

Did you know: It's common to replace the dropped T and D with what is known as a glottal stop. This is where the sound stops in the back of the mouth – similar to a coughing reflex.

The remedy: First, start listening out for the difference. You can do the vocal warm-up to get into practice, and some tongue twisters specific for Ts and Ds. Consciously apply yourself to pronouncing them in the two crucial places, record yourself three times a week reading aloud (any text will do) and listen back for your final and mid-word consonants. You'll soon notice a difference.

PITFALL THREE: MIXING UP CONSONANT SOUNDS

A further consonant pitfall is to switch one consonant sound with another, and there are a few classic culprits. Specifically, mixed consonants happen with the following sounds:

- W and V exchanged (this is often for Indian and Middle Eastern speakers), so wedding becomes vedding.

- TH and F or V exchanged (this is often for south London or cockney speakers), so mother becomes movver.

- NG and K exchanged (this is often for south London or Cockney speakers), so nothing becomes nuffink.

- W and a dark L exchanged (at the end of words like bottle), so bottle becomes bottuw.

These sounds are common in some parts of England, especially saaf (south) London, and can quickly place someone in a certain area or culture, social class and background. This is not necessarily a bad thing, but it is how an accent works. What we are interested in is choice. There is power in choice. If the way we speak is leading people to jump to conclusions about us, we can either fight their assumptions (and many do this very successfully) or we can get some new tools to adjust the way we speak.

I don't believe in adjusting our identity for others, but I am a strong believer that a word is more powerful when said correctly. Whatever your motivation, if you feel you are guilty of any of the pitfalls described above, then there's plenty of work you can do to change it. To adjust a specific sound, we recommend the exercises below.

How To Practise

The principles of how to practise are the same whichever issue you are trying to remedy. You will find precise instructions and examples of words and sentences to use in the next section, or you can make up your own.

- **Isolate the sound you need to make and get used to saying it:** Do this about 10 to 20 times. Really make sure you are hyper-aware of what is going on in your mouth.

You can practise with a mirror, which will help you to make the correct shapes with your mouth and tongue. Then practise with your eyes closed. Both will train your brain more quickly.

- **Put the sound into words and repeat:** Then move on to repeating appropriate words until you have done that maybe ten times. Again, make sure your mouth is making the right shapes and you are saying the word correctly.

- **Make a mini sentence:** Finally, start putting the words into short sentences and do that ten times. Ensure the sounds are accurate. If you find yourself making old mistakes, go back and start again.

- **Try with different words:** When you have mastered those words, do the same with three more words from your list. Do no more than two tricky sounds in one day.

- **Practise all the time:** Also, be aware of using the words correctly in your normal speech.

To take these new sounds into your speech, you need to go to the vocal equivalent of the gym. You can't build muscle by doing a one-off gym session, you have to go regularly. The brain and its uptake of new sounds is much the same; you need to practise at least every other day for five minutes.

- For example, start by making the sound W.

- Then repeat the word WINDOW.

- Finally, repeat I WASHED A WINDOW.

Well done! You have completed your gym session.

LONGER PRACTICE SESSIONS

We recommend you do two or three practice sessions a week of at least 20 minutes. These sessions are about the 'dance' of engaging communication. Use all your intonation techniques on materials that inspire you, be that prose, poetry or world-changing speeches. You might want to use a children's story, a newspaper article, a work document, a simple poem such as 'The Owl and the Pussycat', a complex poem, an inspiring speech or a short presentation. It is a good idea to record yourself three or four times a week and listen back, comparing recordings before and after you have practised.

Practice list (find out how to do all of the steps below in Chapter 3)

- Finding the pauses

- Locating stressed words in sentence

- Finding the stressed syllable of the stressed words

- Justifying the pauses in your units through intonation

- Flowing within the unit, connected speech

- Energising the key words with your intention

- Creating images with your speech

- Using eye contact and gesture to highlight the meaning behind your speech

Make a selection of exercises appropriate to the issue you want to address. A few minutes of practice a day will make a huge difference. You won't need all the exercises.

Vocal Warm-Up

Warm-ups and tongue twisters are great for getting your tongue, lips and palate into gear. This is about working on your tool set (the bits of your instrument that you articulate with). This is particularly useful if you mumble or have a slightly muffled sound. If you are ever accused of being unclear, then a few minutes a day on this will do you the world of good!

This will also help you if you have a lisp or have any other kind of consonant issues. Your tongue is literally a muscle that needs working out to keep it vigorous. Rectify sloppy tongue by doing some warming up – pick a selection from these exercises.

Face, tongue and lips exercises...

Face

- Massage the jaw and face.

- Chew on an imaginary piece of toffee and imagine the toffee getting bigger.

- Make the face as small and then as big as you can. Do this three times.

- Encourage the jaw to loosen by using the heels of the hands to open it and leave it open for a few seconds.

Tongue

- Clean the front and back of every tooth three times using the tongue.

- Point the tongue, holding it still for 10 seconds, then relax the tongue. Repeat three times.

- Place the tip of the tongue behind the bottom teeth and stretch the back of the tongue out as far as it will go, alternating between neutral and stretched out. Repeat ten times.

- Circulate the tongue around the front of the mouth, ten times clockwise and ten times anti-clockwise.

- Stretch the tongue towards the nose, and then the chin. Repeat ten times

- Push the tongue against your index finger, trying to push your finger away. Hold for five seconds and release. Do this five to ten times.

- Go through some consonants at high speed: B, D, G, B, D, G (sounds like budiga very fast), then do the same with p, t, k (putika).

- Now you are going to repeat certain sounds at high speed to make your mouth more dexterous. Make T, D, I, K, G sounds as with T below:

  T t t t   tt tt tt tt   Ttt ttt ttt ttt

  Lll nnn ddd

  Lullaby lollipop

  Manilla vanilla.

Lips

- Place some imaginary bubbles on the ceiling by making a soundless P with the lips – make the sound as crisp as possible. Now do the same thing but add sound to the P.

  Www www www; vvv vvv vvv; bbb bbb bbb.

  Wbw wbw wbw; bwb bwb bwb; wvw wvw wvw; vwv vwv vwv.

- Relax your mouth (or it won't work) and blow through the lips like a horse.
- Make the sounds B, D, G. Make sure they are fully pronounced. Repeat ten times getting faster each time.
- Repeat the same exercise with P, B, M.
- With teeth closed, spread the lips into a smile, and then into a pouting shape. Do this ten times.
- Putting your lips into a pouting shape, close and open them (like a fish). Do this ten times.
- With teeth closed, spread the lips into a smile, and then into a pouting shape. Do this quickly ten times.
- Putting your lips into a pouting shape close, and open them (like a fish). Do this ten times.
- Try this: Whether the weather is cold or whether the weather is hot; we'll weather the weather whatever the weather – whether we like it or not.

Practising with text exercise...

If you continue to practise reading text in different ways and feeling the differences, you will gradually get so much stronger and better.

So now look at the following text from *Under Milk Wood* by Dylan Thomas. Read it out to yourself, taking one instruction at a time.

- Read the passage pronouncing only the consonants, so t, s, spr, n, g is the first phrase.
- Now try over-articulating every word, as if you were talking to a very old, very hard-of-hearing person in a pantomime.
- Try under-articulating, mumbling and speeding through the words and feel the difference.
- Being sure to stay clear and precise, and keeping the neck, jaw and tongue free from tension, repeat the piece super-fast, then super-slow.
- Read it using all the breath with no punctuation. Then read it with punctuation.

- Practise saying a few sentences with your eyes closed. Do this to become aware of the connection points between your tongue and other parts of your mouth.

- Practise saying a few sentences with the knuckle of your thumb in your mouth. Try and speak as clearly as you can, as if you have an audience of 5,000 and your life depends on you being understood. And don't let go of your thumb....

When you have done this, read the same sentences without your thumb. You should hear a massive difference. It works because it forces your mouth to work extra hard, building strength.

To begin at the beginning:

It is Spring, moonless night in the small town, starless and bible-black, the cobble streets silent and the hunched, courters'-and-rabbit's' wood limping invisible down to the sloeblack, slow, black, crowblack, fishingboat-bobbing sea.

The houses are blind as moles (though moles see fine to-night in the snouting, velvet dingles) or blind as Captain Cat there in the muffled middle by the pump and the town clock, the shops in mourning, the Welfare Hall in widows' weeds. And all the people of the lulled and dumbfound town are sleeping now.

Under Milk Wood, *Dylan Thomas*

Finding Your Intention

The above is all well and good, but the most important thing is to find the desire to speak. If your life depended on it, you would make sure you were heard. If your message is stronger than any other belief you hold, you would make sure some fluffiness in the mouth wouldn't get in your way. The psychological approach – if you are mumbling, strengthen your intention.

Make the need to be heard and understood so strong that you will get those words out.

A good way to practise this is to stand in a room, a few centimetres away from the wall. Say a single line to the wall, at the level it needs to be heard. Perhaps your name: 'I am…'

Take a step back and say it again, this time increasing volume so if the wall were a person, it would hear you loud and clear. Keep doing this until you are at the other side of the room, and you feel confident your voice is still hitting the wall loudly and clearly.

Regular practices like this and the mumbling will soon be a thing of the past.

Mixed consonant diagnostic exercise

If you find any of the word combinations below tricky, or think the word pair sounds the same, then you may need some consonant work. Circle the combinations you find difficult.

apple / light ('l' sound)   hard / heart   harm /arm   leisure / ledger
part / path   right / light   right / white   sure / saw   thin / fin
thin / thing   vow / bow   while / vile

WORKING WITH TH – MUVVER OR MOTHER?

For many Londoners, in particular, the TH is a challenge and, as we have learnt, it can be beneficial to have the choice when it comes to accurate consonants.

TH sounds and words exercise...

A simple way to make the TH sound is to begin saying D, D, D (or T, T, T for voiceless TH. With each D, stick your tongue further out until it is protruding from your mouth.

If you are still struggling or if your TH is too harsh, place the tip of your tongue between your teeth and gently blow air through the gap. Imagine your teeth are really sharp so if you press down too hard, you will cut your tongue!

Now start to practise with words instead of sounds.

- The position is to start with the tongue placed between the teeth, slightly sticking out. If you add voice, you get the voiced TH (these, weather), and if you only use breath, you get the voiceless TH (thing, thought). The positioning of the mouth is the same for both. Repeat the words two or three times. Then move to the short sentences.

- TH unvoiced: Three, thirst, thin, thread, hearth, path, thick, thumb, mouth, think, thing.

- TH voiced: This, these, they, there, those, either, bathe, with, soothe, together, that, then.

TH sentences exercise...

Circle the TH sounds in the following sentences, then say them slowly in front of a mirror, looking for the pink of your tongue tip at each TH.

Short Sentences

- There were three thin thieves.
- My mother and father were together on the path.
- Thursday was the day for being thankful.
- There were a thousand things I had thought of.
- He was thrilled with the weather.
- This is the path that is full of heather.
- I think my thread is broken.

Long Sentences

- I saw 'The Thinker' on Thursday in the Netherlands; it is a very famous sculpture of a thinking man, who is in a thoughtful pose.
- The weather in the south of England is healthy and warm and nothing is finer than a Thursday walk with my father and brother.
- Fred the thief of France was famous for his toughness.
- The teacher was terribly nice but I thought she was teaching us things that we didn't ever think about.
- Tom was too thoughtful to take Tricia to the town hall to dance, because her thumb was broken.

THE MIXED-UP L SOUND

Some speakers struggle with what is called the dark L sound. This is the L that comes at the end of words like bottle or little. When it is not pronounced, this sounds lazy. The tongue sits loosely in the mouth and the lips come forward into a w position. So 'well' would sound like 'weoow'.

Mixed-up L sound and word exercise...

The best trick to make this sound is to imagine there is a dot on the roof of your mouth, just behind your top teeth, and also that there is a dot on the tip of your tongue. To make the dark l, put your mouth in the position of the vowel sound OR (as in horse), then bring your tongue tip to the roof of your mouth to meet the dot behind your front teeth. This requires your tongue to come up in a bowl-like shape in your mouth.

Practise with any of these words: *all, apple, beautiful, belt, bill, bottle, candle, capital, cattle, cuddle, feel, full, horrible, mental, middle, needle, pearl, pulls, riddle, sell, settle, subtle, table, tail, tool, wall, world.*

Mixed-up L sentences exercise...

- I always drink bottles of apple juice; they are wonderful.
- Jill cuddles the little girl, and then giggles.
- Pickles go well with ham; treacle goes well with cake.

THE MIXED-UP K OR G SOUND

Losing the precision of the NG sound can really place an accent and stops it from sounding clean and neutral. Again, it's fine if that's what you want, but if you do want to sound more neutral and/or formal, then this sound needs to be corrected.

Mixed-up K and G sound and word exercises...

To make this sound, begin by saying 'anger'. Now just say the first part 'ann' and don't release into the G. And that's your ING sound! The tip of the tongue is low in the mouth and the back of the tongue is high. This sound does not occur at the beginning of words but it does occur between vowels.

Practise with any of these words: *wing, sing, sung, ring, hang, nothing, railing, think, wink, bank, long ago, bring it, longing, banging, sinner, singer, tons, tongues, sun, sung, bun, bung, singin, singing.*

Mixed-up K and G sentence exercises...

- I was thinking how swimming and exercising are as good as shopping or watching movies.
- Paying rent, commuting, eating and drinking, has been taking all the money I was earning from typing, writing and publiciing.
- Without thinking, the king swung on the bell and it rang with a ting-a-ling.
- We are singing a song for spring.

Tongue twisters exercise...

Pick a selection and repeat them more and more quickly as you improve your accuracy.

- Whether the weather is warm or whether the weather is hot. We'll weather the weather whatever the weather, whether we like it or not.
- She sells sea shells on the sea shore. The shells she sells are shells for sure.
- I thought a thought. But the thought I thought wasn't the thought I thought I thought. If the thought I thought I thought had been the thought I thought, I wouldn't have thought so much.
- Freaky Fred found fifty feet of fruit and fed forty feet to his friend Frank. How many feet of fruit did Freaky Fred find?
- A tutor who tooted the flute, tried to tutor two tooters to toot. Said the two to the tutor, 'Is it harder to toot or to tutor two tooters to toot?'
- A good cook could cook as much cookies as a good cook who could cook cookies.
- Betty bought a bit of butter, but the bit of butter made her butter bitter, so Betty bought a better bit of butter than the bit of bitter butter Betty bought before.
- Peter Piper picked a peck of pickled peppers. If Peter Piper picked a peck of pickled peppers, where's the peck of pickled peppers Peter Piper picked?

- Proper copper coffee pot.
- Fuzzy Wuzzy was a bear, Fuzzy Wuzzy had no hair, FuzzyWuzzy wasn't very fuzzy... was he?
- How much wood could a wood chopper chop, if a wood chopper could chop wood?
- Upper roller, lower roller, upper roller, lower roller.
- Round and round the rugged rock the ragged rascal ran.
- Red lorry, yellow lorry, red lorry, yellow lorry.
- His arm was awfully heavy but half hidden by Aunty Helen's head.
- Little Lola loved her lollipops, but lately she has been living in St Lucia, which has no lollies for Lola!
- The apples were a little old, but they still looked beautiful and edible.
- The king was singing a song that rang through the palace and sounded wrong.

You can learn beautiful enunciation
/ GOLDEN RULES /

1. A word without its consonants lacks edges and definitions.

2. Clear enunciation helps you to fit in in any environment.

3. There are three pitfalls with fluffy consonants – mumbling, dropped consonants and mixed consonants.

4. Practice should include a warm-up, tongue twisters and practising sounds.

5. If you practise for five minutes a day for 21 days, you can learn to change old habits and make new ones.

Chapter 18 | Unleash your powerful voice|

In this chapter you will learn about:

- **Aligning your body:** Your voice needs the proper framework
- **Finding the diaphragmatic breath:** Learning to breathe
- **Finding your resonance:** For the ultimate delivery

Our voice is unique and is an important part of how we express ourselves in the world. Yet many people complain that they don't like their voices or they feel that their voices don't represent them. If you think of yourself as an instrument, then – just like a violin or a clarinet – you have to take care of it to make sure it sounds as good as it can. This chapter will give you basic techniques to help you develop your voice, find your vocal resonance, and have access to more vocal impact.

TO BE HEARD CLEARLY AND EFFECTIVELY, a person needs to be physically engaged, and have best use of their vocal instrument. Now while a lot of the power in someone's voice comes from their intention and desire to deliver, there is also some work that you can do physically to ensure your voice is strong, powered by the engine of your body and fuelled by your breath. So if you feel you would like to strengthen your voice so that you can project it outwards, and ensure you've got enough breath to make your points, then I highly recommend you do some of the breathing and vocal work in this chapter. If you find you get into it and/or really feel the need to work on this in more detail, then I recommend further books for you to read at the end of this chapter, or that you work with a coach.

There are four areas within vocal impact, three of which we will cover in this chapter: aligning your body, aligning your breathing and resonance. The fourth area, articulation, we covered in the previous chapter.

Aligning Your Body

Think about your body like a hose – it's going to be difficult to get the full power of the water if there is a kink in the hose. The same with your body,

Scenario: Pitch is important

Imagine this. You're in a meeting with lots of people talking, and then suddenly everyone is quiet because the person on the left has started speaking. You notice his low, full voice and you realise you just enjoy listening to him. He sounds reassuring and intelligent.

The voice does matter. It's not the be all and end all, but it matters.

Now imagine this. You're in a meeting with the new chairwoman. You've heard about her experience, expertise and just how impressive she is, and she certainly looks the part. She is listening intently, really taking it in and she looks like she has something of real value to say.

She opens her mouth to speak.

And out comes a high-pitched squeak of a voice, in no way attached to her diaphragm. This voice does not come from her belly, it comes from her throat. You're taken aback. It just didn't match your expectations. It takes you a while to tune in, but after a few moments, you start to listen to the content, and realise she is really good at her job. But you find yourself wondering how you will listen to her voice every meeting for the next however long. Honestly, if she is a brilliant speaker, it won't take long before we'll forget her voice and take note of what she is saying. But we want her to have a voice to suit her appearance and credentials. And the high pitched squeak doesn't.

you want to get full and easy access to your diaphragm, which is essentially your breath supply. You can see what I mean by just doing a simple exercise now. Put your chin as high in the air as you can, as if you are trying to look at the patch of sky right above your head. Now say 'hello'. Now bring your chin down so it is level. Say 'hello' again. There should be a big difference in vocal quality. When your neck is stretched, you don't have the same access to your diaphragm. Hence the strained voice.

So, to begin, let's look at how you align your body.

YOUR PHYSICAL PRESENCE

Stand up in what feels like a normal position. If you are wearing heels, take them off, so that your feet feel rooted. Now consider each part of your body and observe your natural position.

- Feet: Where is your weight?

- Hips: Are your hips thrust forwards or backwards?
- Spine: Is your spine slumped or held rigidly?
- Shoulders: Are your shoulders rounded or pulled down and back?
- Head: Is there tension?
- Jaw: Is your jaw clenched or unclenched?

FINDING YOUR BODY ALIGNMENT

Now go through again but this time follow the instructions to adjust where necessary so you align your body correctly. Notice if you feel any different.

Feet: Ideally, your feet should be around hip distance apart and your weight should be evenly balanced across both feet and in the toes and heels.

Hips: Your hips should be centred. To find the centre for your hips, put your hands on your hips and thrust your hips forward, as if you are trying to turn your pelvis upwards. Now go in the other direction, thrust your hips backwards and point your bum out, as if you are trying to point your pelvis to point to the floor. Now go for centre, somewhere between both those two points.

Spine: You are aiming for your spine to be aligned and erect. Again, go for the two extremes in order to find a comfortable middle way. Your spine should not be slumped, nor should it be so rigidly held it feels uncomfortable. It should feel an easy sense of alignment. As with the posture section, like there is a string reaching from the top of your head to the sky.

Shoulders: Ensure that your shoulders are relaxed and aligned. Stroke your shoulders back and down, as described in the posture section (see Chapter 7), so hopefully you are familiar.

Head: Make sure your chin is balanced, as if on a table (see Chapter 7).

Jaw: Your jaw should be relaxed. If you are not sure if your jaw is clenched or not, try clenching it and then releasing. If you find you have a habitually clenched jaw, this could certainly inhibit the release of your sounds. Yawning is good, and massaging your face, with particular attention to the jaw, and also stroking the jaw open.

RELEASING TENSION

We can hold a lot of tension in our body and this can get in the way of our coming across physically at ease. It also affects our voice (our body is our instrument after all). Therefore it can be a good thing to do some releasing work if you have a high-pressured speech to make. Below are some good exercises to do. Make sure you have a room to yourself so you don't feel inhibited.

These exercises are directly aiding voice production as all these muscles are connected to the voice box.

Released walking exercise...

Walk quickly as if you have the intention to get somewhere – allow the arms to swing forward. Feel the ground through the whole of each foot. Notice your back, the space around your back, and the space that you occupy. After about 20 seconds, stop and feel alive and alert and ready to communicate.

Released standing exercise...

Release your chin to your chest and roll down your spine so that your upper body is dangling towards the floor. From here, shake out your shoulders. Keep your knees released and let your head hang. Take a breath in this position and notice where you can feel the breath coming in.

Gradually come up – breathing into the small of your back as you do so. Imagine a string at the top of your head. Allow the string to pull the crown of your head up until you are fully in alignment. Let your shoulders fall into place.

Now in a standing position, rock backwards and forwards on your feet to find equal weight placement. Swing your arms out to the side freely – but endeavour to keep the shoulders heavy.

Full body tension release exercise...

- Yawn and stretch, allowing the breath to enter freely and deeply.
- Face stretch – to release facial tension.

- Bear hug to feel the breath enter the ribs and the back.
- Swing the arms and feel their weight, keeping the feet and knees tension-free.
- Do little bounces on the spot, small jumps and shakes.
- Stretch the neck muscles with head and neck stretches.

Finding The Diaphragmatic Breath

Most people tend to breathe high up into their chest, so their ribs move out laterally. This is not necessarily the most efficient way to breathe. There is another kind of breathing called diaphragmatic breathing. This involves breathing deeper and lower in your body, by contracting your diaphragm. By doing this you create room for the lungs to expand down, which means that you can fill up much more of your lungs, get more air and thereby use more of your body as an instrument. Breathing from the diaphragm means that you can not only project your voice further for longer, but that your voice can have additional resonance.

This deep breathing is generally considered a healthier and fuller way to take in oxygen. It's used in yoga and is often used in different kinds of therapies as well, for hyperventilation, anxiety and even stuttering. Just doing five minutes a day is good for you.

DID YOU KNOW?

Five advantages of using the diaphragm

Efficient gas exchange – the bottom third of the lungs is where about two-thirds of the gas exchange takes place, so oxygenation is more efficient when you use the diaphragm.

Less tension and tightness in the neck and shoulders as the muscles there can relax.

Diaphragmatic breathing rebalances the autonomic nervous system, reducing heart rate and breathing rate and changing from sympathetic fight or flight to parasympathetic calm and relax.

Diaphragmatic breathing gently 'massages' or moves the abdominal organs, aiding digestion and helping lymphatic drainage; much of the lymphatic system is located just below the diaphragm.

The diaphragm contributes to good posture and core muscle strength, so needs to work properly. In fact, overdeveloped abs and sucking the stomach in can hinder proper movement of the diaphragm and promote upper chest breathing.[11]

So why don't we do it?

It's thought that the stresses of modern life lead the sympathetic nervous system to be over-stimulated, which means that people carry too much tension in their belly, chest and back. This makes it difficult for the diaphragm to move freely through its full range of motion. It's either that, or we're just not used to it. Actors are trained to use their diaphragm and if you've done a yoga class you've probably had some experience of it. All in all, it's a pretty good life skill.

HOW TO ACHIEVE DIAPHRAGMATIC BREATHING

Working with a relaxed breath can help you in so many ways: harnessing nerves, lowering the pulse rate, supporting the voice. Start with this simple breathing exercise a few times, then move on to the move challenging ones below.

Put a hand on your belly and blow air out for a count of ten. Once you've hit ten, see if you can blow any more air out, and then some more and then hold it until you really have to take a breath.

When you are forced to take a breath, let this happen as your survival reflex rather than consciously. The breath will flood back in and you should feel your belly move outwards. If so, that's diaphragmatic breathing. You probably felt some muscles kicking into action right at the end of the outward breath. Those are your support muscles and they give extra power to your voice. They're pretty useful, too!

You can train yourself so this type of breathing becomes automatic. It will help you build more resonance into your voice and project more. Below are a selection of different exercises to help you achieve this. If you were to spend 15 to 30 minutes practising a selection of these three times a week for a month, you would soon notice a difference.

Breathing and speech exercise...

Use one breath for each line and see which line you can get too. Take a deep breath at the beginning of the sentence and see if you can keep your voice connected and engage your support muscles right up till the final word. Think through to the end of the phrase each time. It's easier if you imagine a point where you are getting the information to, such as the other side of the room.

- I want to know.
- I want to know if you are happy.
- I want to know if you are happy to meet me at ten.
- I want to know if you are happy to meet me at ten, to speak with me.
- I want to know if you are happy to meet me at ten, to speak with me, and if you are.
- I want to know if you are happy to meet me at ten, to speak with me, and if you are we can reach an agreement.

Tip: If you can't feel your support muscles, try pushing against a wall as you say the line.

Finding Your Resonance

We all sound different because of the shape of our resonating cavity – which is our body. It is the same way that a violin and a cello sound different. The sound vibrates in different empty spaces around the body. However, we have some options about where we let our voice resonate. We can 'send' it to different parts of the body.

A rich, resonant voice is a powerful tool for communication, and if you think your voice needs some work, then these exercises are a good place to start. It might be that you will benefit from a bit of help with a coach, but if you are sensitive to your own body and the different sounds and feelings, there's no reason why you can't takes big strides forward at home.

The exercise below is to help you find and build resonance in different areas of your body. It will also help you find tonal range. This is quite technical and may not be necessary for you – but you might well want to try for the fun of it!

Simple resonance exercise...

Make a yawn hum. This is where you yawn, close your lips so the yawn is inside your mouth (you will feel it makes your mouth cavity far more spacious and feels a little odd) and now hum. That's a yawn hum.

Now try and direct your hum into different parts of your body. Let's try a few of the zones below; this is just a selection. Let your tone change if it wants to – that's fine. If there are any words in brackets other than the direction 'yawn hum', say them in that zone as they will help you locate it.

While you are doing this, put your hand in the zone, so rest it on your forehead for zone 4, and after a moment you should start to feel a vibration.

- Zone 1 teeth and lips (yawn hum).

- Zone 2 down into the throat (yawn hum).

- Zone 3 up into the behind the nose (as this produces a nasal sound we'll use some words here – try saying naughty nora – it should sound very nasal!).

- Zone 4 forehead (yawn hum).

- Zone 5 skull (yawn hum).

- Zone 6 chest (as this produces a chesty sound a yawn hum won't work from the chest, simply make a chesty ho ho ho).

Now direct an 'OO' sound into the same areas. Some areas will be easier than others and you may not notice a big difference between them.

Now speak a couple of months of the year in each of these zones and note the difference in sound quality.

Well done! This is how you build resonance in different areas!

QUESTIONS TO PONDER

- When you say a few words in each of these zones, can you hear the different sound quality?

- How do you feel?

- Who might speak like this (a famous person)? And in what situation? Where, for example, does Daniel Craig speak? And how about Donald Trump?

- When you yawn hum through your pitch range, which zone vibrates more?

- Where do you mainly speak from (chest / throat / nasal area etc)?

Resonance and text exercise...

Have a look at the text below. It is a short extract from a children's story which requires plenty of different vocal qualities to communicate it effectively. Have a read of it as you would normally and record it. Now look at it with the intention of exploring some of the different aspects we have looked at in this section.

Have fun with the text, and try different aspects each time:

- Sustaining your breath to the end of the line.

- Exploring sounds. First, try the shape of the vowel sounds – just whispering through and then sounding just the vowels within the text. Then explore the crispness and dynamism of each individual consonant.

- Then on full voice – exploring the different vocal qualities you could employ. Try and give a different voice to each of the characters, maybe one will be very nasal and another very chest resonant. See if you can make this come alive using the full range of your voice to tell the story.

Goldilocks and the three bears

Once upon a time, there was a little girl named Goldilocks. She went for a walk in the forest. Pretty soon, she came upon a house. She knocked and, when no one answered, she walked right in.

At the table in the kitchen, there were three bowls of porridge. Goldilocks was hungry. She tasted the porridge from the first bowl.

'This porridge is too hot!' she exclaimed.

So she tasted the porridge from the second bowl.

'This porridge is too cold,' she said

So she tasted the last bowl of porridge.

'Ahhh, this porridge is just right,' she said happily and she ate it all up.

Goldilocks was very tired by this time, so she went upstairs to the bedroom. She lay down in the first bed, but it was too hard. Then she lay in the second bed, but it was too soft. Then she lay down in the third bed and it was just right. Goldilocks fell asleep.

As she was sleeping, the three bears came home.

'Someone's been eating my porridge,' growled the Papa bear.

'Someone's been eating my porridge,' said the Mama bear.

'Someone's been eating my porridge and they ate it all up!' cried the Baby bear.

They decided to look around some more and when they got upstairs to the bedroom, Papa bear growled, 'Someone's been sleeping in my bed,'

'Someone's been sleeping in my bed, too' said the Mama bear

'Someone's been sleeping in my bed and she's still there!' exclaimed Baby bear.

Just then, Goldilocks woke up and saw the three bears. She screamed, 'Help!' And she jumped up and ran out of the room and ran away into the forest. And she never returned to the home of the three bears.

QUESTIONS TO PONDER

- What effect did a high voice have?
- What effect did a low voice have?
- In which situations might we want to use a high voice?
- In which situations might we want to use a lower voice?

If you feel you particularly need and want more range and resonance to your voice, then I would suggest you practise a selection of the body, breathing and resonance exercises above, about three times a week, for at least 15 minutes a time, if possible. It sounds like a lot, but you will very quickly start to notice changes.

Essentially, you want to be working in your natural range with your voice. If you think your voice is too high and want to lower it, that is fine, but what you don't want to do is force your voice lower than your natural range as then it will sound awkward and unnatural.

Unleash your powerful voice
/ GOLDEN RULES /

1. In order to have access to your full voice, your body needs to be in alignment. It's difficult to find your vocal resonance if you are hunched over, for example.

2. Practising diaphragmatic breathing is a good way to develop more vocal power, and there are lots of other benefits, too!

3. Remember that we are talking about muscles here – so you need to practise to notice shifts in your voice.

4. Playing with intention – I want to sustain this sound / sentence / numbers all the way to the other side of the wall – will help you find and activate your diaphragmatic and intercostal muscles.

5. Your body is made up of different vocal cavities with different areas of resonance, and you can access and develop each of them in the process building your resonance and range.

Chapter 19
| Conclusion - The biggest communication mistakes and how to avoid them |

In this chapter you will learn about:

- What you say: And what not to say
- What your body says: Give-away body language to avoid
- What your voice says: Make your message loud and clear

To round things up, I thought it would be useful to draw your attention to some of the things to avoid when you are communicating with colleagues and friends, divided into verbal, non-verbal and vocal themes. I wish you so much luck with your ever-improving communication. Remember, it's a lifetime's journey and will add a wonderful richness to your relationships.

What You Say

Avoid 'you' phrases in confrontation situations: These can antagonise your sparring partner and slip them straight into the defensive. Instead of telling them what they did, refer to how it makes you feel.

Avoid to many 'I's in emails – makes you sound self-centred: A well-established theatre director I once wrote to back in my theatre days finally responded to my hounding emails and met me for lunch. After an hour of excellent conversation, he dropped the bombshell. 'You repeated 'I' 37 times in your email,' he said. (Ever since then, the mistake of the most famous pro-noun has been assiduously avoided by myself.)

Avoid talking in interviews without knowing where you are going: You never want the interviewer to wish the ground would swallow them up while you rattle on, trapped in a story that you no longer know why you are telling but feel you can't get out of.

Avoid being generalist and too safe: Instead, bring yourself and your personal experiences, anecdotes, values and stories into your communication. There is room for that bit of you everywhere, from the one-to-one meeting to the public speech and everything in between.

What Your Body Says

Avoid crossed arms: This is not a powerful position, just a closed one. It makes people feel as though you are shut off and removed from the situation. Instead, hold your hands at your navel or hang them at your sides or – if they really feel like a couple of dangly things attached to your shoulders – you can place one in your pocket, or hold a notebook.

Avoid slumped shoulders: Especially when entering a room or starting a speech or presentation, this posture gives a negative impression – and that first impression is crucial! Instead, roll your shoulders back or stroke them open with your fingers. That tiny difference makes a disproportionate improvement and is worth it.

Avoid limp handshakes: Who wants to hold a dead fish? Instead, go firm. Put your enthusiasm to make this new communication relationship into your hand and shake with confidence and conviction. You will have goals from every conversation – it might be as simple as a job, impressing the person, or just to enjoy connecting with someone new. Whatever the goal is, let it be purposeful, and let that be reflected in your hand.

Avoid breaking eye contact: Eye contact can feel scary and revealing, and yet avoiding it is even more revealing. If you can't look someone in the eye, you are effectively giving them licence to think all sorts of things about you that you have no control over.

Avoid clenching your jaw, gritting your teeth or frowning: Unless you want the other person to mirror your body language – in which case they will get defensive or shut down themselves – always avoid these negative signals. It's a bit like a poker player's tell. You need to know what signals you are giving so you can be in control of them. Instead, do a big yawn, relax your mouth, smile to get those muscles working, imagine the warm sun is on your face. Take on an attitude of receptivity and openness, and let your face reflect it. Usually this will benefit you. At the very least, your cards will be held more tightly to your chest.

Avoid fiddling in meetings or interviews; again, it's like displaying your emotions on a screen for people to see: Instead, make sure you are grounded and centred on the chair, using the floor to support you and give you energy. Use your hands to gesticulate as feels natural.

What Your Voice Says

Avoid speaking too fast at the pace of your thoughts: You only get to do this when you are enunciating with utmost clarity and when you have your audience or listeners firmly with you, running alongside you in the frenzied adrenalin of the moment.

Avoid a monotone: Don't drag your voice along as if you have no energy to pull it off the floor. Again, if you do that, people will feel like you don't care about what you are saying.

Avoid long, complicated sentences: Don't put too many clauses in a thought and go up at the end of each one. Instead, use vocal gravity and unit breaks to deliver each mini idea.

Avoid making all words equal: Try not to pronounce grammatical words with the same emphasis that you use for emphasised words. Instead, find the key words that hold your meaning and put your energy in those!

Avoid mumbling or under-articulating: Your audience want to hear what you say without straining. Instead, do your vocal warm-ups and practise speaking clearly with your knuckle in between your teeth!

Avoid barely opening your mouth when you speak: Incarcerating the soul of your words inside your mouth will achieve nothing. Instead, open your mouth and release the emotion around the vowels of the words that are important to you.

AUTHORS NOTE

As you have made your way through this book, I hope you have let it change you, just a little bit, and work some of its magic from the inside out.

I imagine, writing this, that there are all kinds of ways that people can engage with this book, but my sincere hope is that those of you who have read it with the real intention of growing a little, learning something to help you on your journey to being your bigger, better self, have found at least a little bit of magic to make it worthwhile. I'm aware that in this age of multimedia stimulation, sound bites and video clips, one's attention span has shrunk, and so it has been my intention to write something that can be read cover to cover or dipped into and still give something special and high quality to its readers. I hope you have tried some (or even all) of the various exercises, perhaps practised warm-ups, vocal impact, a new posture, and that you have let it really change how you deliver presentations.

I also want to add that I have learnt a great deal while writing this book. In fact, all the LSW team have. I had a funny time writing the defusing conflict chapters, as I was dealing with a conflict of my own and struggling with the flow of the text. It took me a few days to realise I needed to practise the methods I was writing about, and it was only then that my writer's block was freed and I could finish the chapters. So learning about communication really is a life project, one that will not finish when this book is closed and worn and leafed through on your shelf, or when it is a dusty manuscript in my office, but one we all go on for a long time. I am thrilled to share the journey with you.

Please do get in touch via email, info@londonspeechworkshop.com, if anything in the book impacted you in any way, helped you grow in confidence, win the perfect job, find peace in a challenging situation. I would be so delighted to hear of your journey.

ENDNOTE

1. Listen at: http://www.youtube.com/watch?v=s1Ulz-Qwnx8

2. This is adapted from a blog by Steven Aitchison: http://www.stevenaitchison.co.uk/blog

3. Sourced from www.scielo.br

4. http://psychcentral.com/blog/archives/2010/11/30/smile-big-youre-going-to-havea-good-long-life/

5. http://www.psypost.org/2013/06/people-anticipate-others-genuine-smiles-but-notpolite-smiles-18420

6. Watch the Youtube clip here: https://www.youtube.com/watch?v=7ffbFvKlWqE
   Read the full article here: http://www.huffingtonpost.com/2013/08/08/billclinton_n_3718956.html

7. http://www.bbc.co.uk/news/uk-politics-24424332

8. Watch it on YouTube: https://www.youtube.com/watch?v=D1R-jKKp3N

9. Source: http://www.storyboardthat.com

10. https://www.youtube.com/watch?v=WibmcsEGLKo

11. Adapted from http://www.breathingremedies.co.uk/2014/07/23/five-health-benefits-of-breathing-with-your-diaphragm/

PHOTO CREDITS

Figure 1.1: https://static.pexels.com/photos/2281/man-personpplp-suit-united-states-of-america.jpg

Figure 1.3: http://s1.1zoom.net/big0/380/364847-svetik.jpg

Figure 1.4: https://images.unsplash.com/photo-1442473483905-95eb436675f1?ix-lib=rb-0.3.5&q=80&fm=jpg&crop=entropy&s=8a25776c0f9340b38d567c-53870da02f

Figure 6.1: https://www.flickr.com/photos/dcoetzee/5535024300

Figure 6.3: Bryan Stevenson at TED2012: Full Spectrum, February 27 - March 2, 2012. Long Beach, James Duncan Davidson. Credit: James Duncan Davidson

Figure 6.4: Credit for Benedict Cumberbatch: Gage Skidmore

Figure 6.6: http://foter.com/f/photo/8432939866/b44f336c24/

Figure 6.9: Credit: Blue Mountain Library

Figure 7.1: Credit: Kennedy Garrett

Figure 7.2: Attributed: Richard Elzey Website: www.visualhunt.com

Figure 7.5: https://pixabay.com/en/martin-luther-king-jr-i-have-a-dream-393870/

Figure 8.1 to Figure 8.6: Tony Blair, Credit: Mark Mueller

For further information please visit

www.londonspeechworkshop.com

Made in the USA
Columbia, SC
11 March 2018